COPING WITH MISCONDUCT IN THE COLLEGE CLASSROOM:
A Practical Model

By Gerald Amada, Ph.D.

Michael Clay Smith, J. D., Ed.D., LL.M., Legal Consultant

CENTER FOR TEACHING EXCELLENCE
Canisius College

The Higher Education Administration Series
Edited by Donald D. Gehring and D. Parker Young

COLLEGE ADMINISTRATION PUBLICATIONS, INC.

College Administration Publications, Inc.,
830 Fairview Road, Suite D, Asheville, NC 28803-1081

© 1999 College Administration Publications, Inc.,
All rights reserved. Published 1999
Printed in the United States of America

Library of Congress Cataloging-in-Publication Data

Amada, Gerald.
    Coping with misconduct in the college classroom : a practical
model / by Gerald Amada ; Michael Clay Smith, legal consultant.
       p.   cm. — (The higher education administration series)
    Includes index.
    ISBN 0-912557-23-0
    1. College discipline—United States.   2. Counseling in higher
education—United States.   I. Smith, Michael Clay.   II. Title.
III. Series.
LB2344.A477   1999
378.1'95—dc21   98–33175
                                             CIP

To Ami and Robert Amada
And Jacob Ehrlich

Contents

About the Author • *vii*

About the Legal Consultant • *ix*

Introduction • *xi*

I. **Common Disruptive Classroom Behaviors** • 1
Grandstanding • 1
Sleeping in Class • 2
Prolonged Chattering • 3
Excessive Lateness • 3
Poor Personal Hygiene • 4
Overt Inattentiveness • 5
Eating, Drinking, Gum Chewing, Carrying Pagers and
Beepers, and Passing Notes • 5
Unexcused Exits from Class • 6
Verbal or Physical Threats, to Students or Faculty • 7
Disputing the Instructor's Authority and Expertise • 7

II. **Sources of Doubt and Indecision** • 9
"Benign" Inaction • 9
Fears of Receiving Inadequate Administrative Support • 10
Fear of Harming the Psychologically Fragile Student • 12
Fear of Physical or Legal Reprisals • 14
Guilt as a Deterrent to Action • 17
Misperceiving the Nature of Discipline • 19

III. **Principles and Strategies** • 21
The Code of Student Conduct • 22
Forewarning Students in the Course Syllabus • 23
The Principle of Proportionality • 24

Procedures for Reporting Disruptive Incidents • 25
Documentation • 26
Graduated Disciplinary Measures • 30
Acts of Criminality and Slander • 32
Extenuating Circumstances • 34
Dealing with the Disruptive, Disabled Student • 36
Discipline or Therapy? • 38
The Co-Dependent Instructor • 43

IV. **Non-Disciplinary Responses to Classroom Misconduct • 47**
Going the Extra Mile • 47
A Sense of Humor • 49
Teaching Interestingly • 50

V. **Everything You've Always Wanted to Know About Classroom Misconduct and Were Afraid to Ask Your Dean • 55**

About the Author

Dr. Gerald Amada is one of the founders and a director of the Mental Health Program, City College of San Francisco. He also has a private psychotherapy practice in Mill Valley, California. He received the M.S.W. degree at Rutgers University and Ph.D. in social and clinical psychology at the Wright Institute, Berkeley, California. He has published seven books and over fifty articles, book reviews, and booklets on the subjects of mental health, psychotherapy, and disruptive student issues. His latest books are *A Guide to Psychotherapy* (Ballantine Books/Random House), *The Mystified Fortune-Teller and other Tales from Psychotherapy* (Madison Books), and *The Power of Negative Thinking* (Madison Books). In 1994, Dr. Amada published *Coping with the Disruptive College Student: A Practical Model.* He has lectured on over fifty campuses throughout the United States and Canada on the subject of the disruptive college student for the past fifteen years. He has also been a keynote speaker at bi-national and regional conferences held in Montreal, New Orleans, Worcester, Cape Cod, Baltimore, Asilomar, and Sacramento.

Dr. Amada has been a book reviewer for the American Journal of Psychotherapy, University Press of America, the San Francisco Chronicle, and the Journal of College Student Psychotherapy. He is a member of the editorial board and is the book review editor of the last-mentioned journal. He is the recipient of the 1984 Award of Excellence in the category of administrator, Post Secondary Education, conferred by the National Education Special Needs Personnel, Region 5, which comprises 18 states.

Dr. Amada enjoys and feels challenged by the opportunity to develop principles, strategies and guidelines for promoting civility on the college campus.

About the Legal Consultant

Dr. Michael Clay Smith is Professor of Criminal Justice and Education Administration at the University of Southern Mississippi.

His background includes many years of experience as an administrator and attorney for institutions of higher education.

He is author of three books, including *Coping with Crime on Campus* (Macmillan, 1988), and more than thirty articles in legal, education and criminology journals. He holds degrees in law from Tulane Law School and Mississippi College, and a doctorate in higher education administration from West Virginia University.

Introduction

Incidents of disruption in college classrooms on campuses throughout the United States and Canada are legion and multiform, according to the firsthand reports I have received from many colleagues, faculty and non-faculty alike, over the past twenty years or so.

I first became aware of the magnitude of this problem on my own campus when a significant number of faculty enlisted my services as a consultant while in the throes of a crisis involving a disruptive student who perplexed, stymied or, quite often, frightened them. Although, initially, I had no formal training and certainly little expert knowledge in the specialized area of student discipline, I discovered that quite often I could be helpful to my colleagues by providing them with a combination of emotional support (primarily by commiserating and identifying with their plight) and some practical advice as to how best to approach the offending student.

Admittedly, I was using a seat-of-the-pants approach that was fraught with potential pitfalls, largely because I was unfamiliar with the legal requirements and administrative precedents that governed the proper utilization of disciplinary interventions on the college campus. Because I was slowly gaining among my colleagues a slightly deserved reputation for being a reliable resource and "resolver" of disruptive crises, I felt compelled to learn as much as I could about the myriad contributors—individual, social, and institutional—to student disruptiveness. As well, I became determined to acquire a breadth of practical skills and knowledge that would enable me to help others resolve disruptive incidents, quickly, legally, and satisfactorily.

The first conundrum I faced was the question of why there was such a burgeoning rise in disruptive incidents on my campus. Was this disquieting social phenomenon peculiar to my college (City College of San Francisco, an urban community college) or to urban colleges in general? Were community colleges, in particular, with their open admissions policies, especially susceptible to and beleaguered by disruptive students? Was student disruptiveness part and symptomatic of a larger social phenomenon, the general rending of the moral fiber of our society and, to borrow a phrase used by Anna Freud, the widespread decline in the authority of the conscience?

Over the ensuing years I have garnered partial, imprecise answers to some of these questions. I have discovered from visiting over fifty colleges and universities—urban, suburban, and rural, public and private, two- and four-year—in both Canada and the United States, that the vast majority of schools are highly pervious to students who engage in misconduct, often of a highly offensive, disruptive, and even dangerous nature. This misconduct takes many forms and surfaces in virtually every occupiable facility of the college. Occasionally, it is true, administrators from rural, fairly isolated colleges, will inform me by phone or at conferences that their colleges are, thankfully, quite immune from the influences of disruptive students. Invariably, they conceded, usually rather bemusedly, that they are keeping their fingers tightly crossed because they expect that within the next decade or so they will be in "the same boat" as most other colleges.

A second question I asked myself in the early years of consulting with faculty about disruptive students was why I, in particular, was being sought by them for help. After all, my college already had in place an institutional disciplinary system for dealing with student disruptiveness, including a broad panoply of codes, procedures and administrative personnel fine-tuned for the specific purpose of trouble-shooting and resolving disruptive incidents on campus. Why, then, were these faculty complainants not simply adhering to and utilizing the disciplinary system available to all college personnel? There were several answers to this question, but two had conspicuously leaped out at me, time and time again.

First, most of the faculty who sought my services had already attempted to receive assistance from designated college administrators and, alas, had met with unsatisfactory results. They encountered unexpected and adverse responses when they reported incidents involving disruptive students to administrators. One response they commonly received was a snorting, light-hearted, dismissive suggestion to temporize or ignore the problem with the reassurance that it would somehow spontaneously resolve itself without the benefit of administrative intervention. Even when the disruptive crisis had already reached frightening or dangerous proportions they were sometimes advised to return to the classroom to stoically endure unbearable emotional pressure in an untenable academic environment. Worse, administrators not

Coping with Misconduct in the College Classroom

only refused to act affirmatively to resolve disruptive crises, but would punitively intimate or even explicitly state that the reported incident of disruption was the fault of the instructor who had instigated it through culpable acts of malice or ineptitude even when this was manifestly untrue. Small wonder that faculty were feeling disillusioned, bitter, and demoralized over the way in which the college was mismanaging cases of student disruptiveness and had developed a rigid aversion to reporting their complaints to those administrators who were officially responsible for dealing with disciplinary matters on campus.

I think it apt to mention here, parenthetically, that the present core of administrators who are designated to deal with discipline at my college are, unlike some of their predecessors, knowledgeable, resolute, and extremely competent in dealing with disruptive students and, as a result, staff are far more confident and forthcoming in requesting administrative intervention in cases of student disruption. As a result, today's City College of San Francisco campus is a much safer and more viable environment for staff and students.

The second reason complainants were bypassing administrators and submitting their reports to me was more ambiguous. Gradually, I came to learn that many of the instructors who had been confronted by highly disruptive students were formulating quixotic ideas about involving me and the Mental Health Program in plans of action that were both ethically questionable and positively counterproductive. Their thinking took the following syllogistic course: Since the disruptive student was engaging in a form of behavior that was definably aberrant, the student was, *ipso facto*, a disturbed person. Being a disturbed person, the disruptive student required psychological treatment. The most likely and logical place for this treatment was the City College of San Francisco Mental Health Program since it was conveniently located and there was no fee for service.

There were additional premises underlying this line of reasoning: Since the disruptive students were demonstrably psychologically disturbed persons, they could never have received treatment in the past nor were they receiving treatment at the time of their disruptiveness (such premises were usually found to be false upon further investigation). These students, if there were some palatable way to refer them to the Mental Health Program, would voluntarily, eagerly and beneficially utilize its services (also found to be a false premise, upon further investigation, in most cases). Finally, the complainants assumed, the disruptive students' utilization of the Mental Health Program would yield a greater corrective and rehabilitative benefit to them and the college than would the imposition of discipline. This premise, considering its pursuit of a kinder, gentler procedure than discipline, might be dubbed a (George) Bushian form of thinking that entailed certain fundamental misconceptions about the nature of both psychotherapy and discipline. For example, the complainants sometimes held the viewpoint that psychotherapy, on the one hand, provided duck soup remedies for disruptiveness and rational, proportionate limit-setting, on the other hand, did not; quite assailable premises to say the least, on both practical and theoretical grounds.

I also discovered in my consultations with these colleagues that often they were not loathe to recommend the coercive use of psychotherapy in dealing with disruptive students. Quite frequently, even the most compassionate, idealistic, and fair-minded of my colleagues somehow had no ethical qualms about using some form of force, manipulation, cajolery, or artifice to engineer disruptive students into psychotherapy; if necessary, against the students' wishes. When I demurred, as I always did in such situations, there was often a response of disappointment, rationalized by the opinion that disruptive students, even if they participated in therapy involuntarily, would ultimately derive, by hook or crook, some benefit from the experience. Therefore, the ethical implications of imposing mandatory psychotherapy, they suggested, could be rightfully downplayed or even dismissed.

These consultations generally took a very positive, constructive turn, however, when I invited my colleagues to consider utilizing the already-in-place codes of student conduct to resolve disruptive incidents. After all, the codes were specific, clear, comprehensive and legally enforceable. Practically every conceivable form of disruptive behavior was governed and proscribed by the existing codes. If one followed due process procedures—providing sufficient warnings to students, documenting incidents, etc.—most of these disruptive crises, it seemed to me, could be resolved quickly, thoroughly, and in a legally acceptable manner. Rather than fruitlessly delve into a large, complex morass of psychiatric considerations and criteria, I recommended that faculty clearly and specifically identify the nature of the disruptive behavior(s), link these behaviors to a specific code of student conduct, carefully document their findings, and transmit their reports to the proper college authorities. Throughout the process I avidly remained in their corner by offering advice, information, and emotional support until the crisis was resolved.

As more and more faculty became conversant and comfortable with the methods of identifying and reporting incidents of disruption, it became clear to me that the managing of disruptive conduct on the college campus was a teachable and highly important skill. Although I still considered my knowledge of the subject to be rather scanty, I decided to write a journal article in which I outlined certain practical and theoretical considerations for dealing with disruptive students. A year or two later I was contacted by a university in Montreal, Canada, inviting me to appear as the keynote speaker at a binational conference on disruption and violence on the contemporary college campus. When I

Coping with Misconduct in the College Classroom

inquired as to why I, in particular, was selected for this distinction, I was told that, after scouring the corpus of literature related to the disruptive college student, their staff found only **one** article, mine!

I was pleased, flattered and quite shocked by this discovery. I had not bothered to research the subject very much when I had written my article so had little idea what scholars and practitioners had written about it in the past. Evidently, according to my informants, very little. It was then that I fully realized that I was entering uncharted but very fertile terrain by investigating the subject of the so-called disruptive college student. At the Montreal conference and at other college conferences I attended, I discovered that practically every category of college employee—administrators, instructors, nurses, psychotherapists, counselors, support staff—was deeply and regularly impacted by students who were disruptive and, as a result, was evincing a great need for practical help in dealing with this problem. In short, I realized that the problem of the disruptive college student was a national phenomenon and one that had already reached serious, if not dangerous, proportions.

Given the general alarum I discerned among so many of my colleagues in Canada and the United States, I decided to write another article on the subject, and, with some well-deserved prodding from my wife, Marcia, I expanded my findings into a book, *Coping with the Disruptive College Student: A Practical Model.* This book has been well received and, according to many of my readers, serves effectively as a practical aid with which to understand and resolve disruptiveness on campus.

Soon after publishing this book, however, I discovered that I had made a thoughtless and important oversight. Although the book deals rather thoroughly with the subject of the disruptive student, its approach is rather generic and global. After lecturing to faculty audiences at many conferences in recent years, I have come to realize that the classroom setting in particular is an academic milieu in which a vast amount and variety of misconduct takes place, and for this reason it deserves special consideration in any serious study of disruptiveness on the college campus.

With this oversight in mind, I have written this book as a corrective, an emendation to the earlier book, to make amends, so to speak. I hope it will serve its readers well in their pursuit of academic excellence. This book is dedicated with love to two devoted teachers, my niece and nephew, Amy and Robert Amada, who are very special to me. It is also dedicated with love to my grandson, Jacob Ehrlich, who, because he was a bit of a slowpoke about entering our family, was not included in an earlier dedication.

Gerald Amada, Ph.D   San Francisco

Chapter I

Common Disruptive
Classroom Behaviors

As indicated in the introduction, disruptive behaviors in the classroom take many forms and seem to be delimited only by the antic imaginations of their perpetrators. Instructors throughout the country are discerning a marked behavioral trend among their students manifested in crass incivility toward others, self-indulgent demands and expectations, and an implacable contempt for others, particularly those in positions of institutional authority such as the instructors themselves. Interpersonal rudeness, according to some university officials, is the prevailing idiom of social communication, a kind of *lingua franca* of the college campus. Clearly, these unflattering characterizations do not befit or apply to the majority of students, most of whom behave respectfully toward both college officials and their peers. However, each year, it seems, larger numbers of students are engaging in behaviors that frighten and confound instructors, contaminate the academic climate of the classroom, and make genuine learning and teaching unattainable goals.

In this chapter we will simply identify, define, and describe those disruptive behaviors that most commonly beset the college instructor. In a subsequent chapter we will deal with the matter of principles, strategies and interventions for resolving disruptive incidents.

GRANDSTANDING

A common plaint of instructors relates to the matter of students who use the classroom to grandstand, monopolizing class discussion by speaking protractedly and bombastically on their favorite subject, with blithe disregard for the possible irrelevancy of their comments. Some students attempt to bask in the attention they receive from their academic peers (even when that attention is rancorous) for their

1

self-perceived intellectual brilliance, knowledge, or forensic skills. It is quite common for some students to use the classroom as a forum for their exalted political ideology, speaking lengthily about the social and political ills of society in courses where there is virtually no political content or interest. Other students, entirely oblivious to the rights and needs of others, use the classroom as a launching pad to regale their peers with tales of their personal lives, including, at times, intimate tidbits that are neither germane nor savory considering the academic milieu in which they are disclosed. In any event, some students seem driven by a sense of self-importance that impels them to pontificate and monopolize classroom discussions. Instructors who do not cope adequately with this problem usually discover that they and their students will become demoralized under the deadly influence of students who monologue.

SLEEPING IN CLASS

At first glance, the problem of student slumberers seems frivolous or trivial. After all, these students are merely catnapping and, assuming they are not snoring loudly, they distract or disturb no one. But, is that really the case? I think not. The student who sleeps in class is a veritable disruption, albeit one of a passive type. The classroom sleeper represents a problem for several reasons.

First, students who are allowed to sleep in class create a quandary for everyone. They are obviously not interested or participating in the academic tasks at hand, whether these tasks are lectures or discussions. What does such oblivious non-participation represent to other students who are conducting themselves more attentively? If an instructor ignores the sleeping student, a tacit communication of some import is unwittingly conveyed. That communication, intended or not, carries the sorry message that intellectual acuity, involvement and participation carry no more value than intellectual somnolence. Since most instructors rightly value the opportunity to inspire and engage students in the process of intellectual dialogue and inquiry, it makes no sense to disregard the student who flouts their dedicated efforts by sleeping in the classroom.

Second, the act of sleeping in class should ordinarily be regarded as disrespectful, if not contemptuous, of the instructor as well as of other students. Of course it is true that many students have valid reasons for feeling tired and sleepy: wee-hours cramming for an exam or paper, young children who have nocturnal demands and must be taken to school very early in the morning, an after-school job that lasts into the late evening, etc. As callous as it sounds, these students, like all others, should be expected, at the minimum, to remain awake throughout the duration of the class session. If they cannot, for whatever reason, do so, they should either not attend class on that day or, if they do attend, should unobtrusively leave before nodding off. To use the classroom as one might use his or her dormitory bedroom is insulting to others and therefore should be regarded as unacceptable behavior.

PROLONGED CHATTERING

It is quite common for small cliques of two or three students to engage in private conversations during classroom lectures or discussions. Some of these conversations, on the one hand, may very well relate to the topic under discussion and therefore might be regarded as both germane and consequential. Other such conversations, on the other hand, are clearly of a frivolous nature and bear no relationship whatsoever to the coursework at hand. Whether students are chattering among themselves about some aspect of the course itself or are discussing their private social pastimes and interests, this form of behavior is rude and inappropriate and should therefore be regarded as disruptive and unacceptable.

EXCESSIVE LATENESS

As an occasional guest lecturer at my own college, I am continually struck by the fact that large numbers of students arrive to class excessively late. It is, I have found, not unusual for only one-half the students to be in their seats at the official starting time of the class. Many students arrive 15–30 minutes late, seem to have few compunctions about their tardiness and, to compound the infraction, some enter class with a certain amount of noisy fanfare, waving to friends, walking directly in front of the lecturing instructor without an apology, and loudly arranging their belongings before seating themselves. To make matters worse, many instructors, in my experience, seem to tolerate this form of disruption, winking at it with a sense of futility and bemusement, even though they secretly abhor and resent students who are chronically late.

Tardiness is often rationalized and excused by instructors for a variety of reasons. Students proffer many "legitimate" reasons for their lateness: transportation snags, long distances between classes, last-minute commitments to other urgent matters, etc. Instructors may not wish to assert their prerogatives to insist upon punctuality when faced with students who plead for clemency based upon such unforseen circumstances. Perhaps some instructors have already become so inured to the problem of student tardiness that they no longer consider it important and, therefore, do not believe that requirements regarding punctuality are desirable, achievable, or enforceable.

The desirability and importance of punctuality were stressed by one instructor at my own college. To exemplify his point, he analogized students' attending a class to theatergoers' attending a play at the theater. He pointed out that theater officials generally and strictly prohibit theatergoers from entering the auditorium after the play has begun. This time-honored practice is enforced in deference to the actors and to the audience who would be distracted by the late arrivals, thereby diminishing both the quality of the performance and the pleasure of the playgoers. This instructor pursuasively argued that the college classroom should be considered at least as important as a theater play and therefore should be accorded as much respect. For this reason, he is less tolerant toward unpunctual students and academically penalizes them for excessive lateness.

In my own view, most instances of lateness are avoidable, providing, of course, that students take the requisite precautions to arrive punctually: beginning the journey to class at an earlier time (to allow for unforeseen delays), putting aside other, less pressing, demands in order to be punctual, and generally considering their punctual attendance to be of the utmost importance. Of course, many students are not apt to take such precautions spontaneously. Therefore, instructors much be prepared to set reasonable but firm standards regarding punctuality and must also be prepared to enforce those standards, at times, even when students present highly convincing justifications for their tardiness. It is well to keep in mind that a highly laissez-faire approach to chronic or excessive lateness inevitably condones this practice and sends a message to all students, the punctual and unpunctual alike, that lateness is a trivial matter that is best overlooked. This, unquestionably, is a deleterious message that no conscientious instructor should be imparting to students.

POOR PERSONAL HYGIENE

There is certainly no reason for instructors to expect students to attend class in a condition of impeccable cleanliness. However, there are times when the personal hygiene of certain students requires some assessment and intervention by instructors. The student who only rarely is forgetful and careless about hygiene may not pose much of a problem. Perhaps such a student has just worked up a serious sweat on the athletic field or in a long run to the classroom and has had no opportunity to clean up and get rid of body odor. Other students may be offended and put off by this student for the day but if the student's offensiveness is a one-time matter, there is probably little cause for concern.

There is a type of unhygienic student, however, who does warrant concern and intervention. Such students are completely oblivious to the slovenliness and stench with which they present themselves. There are cases of highly stenchful students who day after day come to class oblivious to their own personal noisomeness. Some of their classmates somehow simply endure the noxious odors, others may retreat and find seats out of noseshot, and still others, I've been told, actually drop the course rather than endure olfactory agony. It is quite remarkable to think that a single student's bodily stench could actually cause the attrition of a class, yet such incidents occur in surprisingly large numbers on our nation's campuses.

Chronic and severe personal insanitariness is a disruptive behavioral problem that violates the rights of both students and instructors. Therefore, students whose strong bodily odors undermine the ability of teachers to teach and students to learn must be confronted about their unacceptable behavior. Because of the sensitive nature of this problem (after all, not even close personal friends or relatives find it easy to share their displeasure over this matter with offenders), many faculty shun this responsibility. In a later chapter I will outline a set of interventions with which to deal with the severely unhygienic student.

OVERT INATTENTIVENESS

There are students who find it extremely difficult to mentally attend to the everyday activities of the classroom, whether it is a lecture or a discussion that is taking place at the time. Some students engage in woolgathering, sitting vacuously in their seats in a state of inertia and stupefaction. Although they will probably not derive much enlightenment from their enrollment in the class, chances are, they will not be disruptive to others. However, some students have a predilection for being ostentatious and arrogant in their display of inattention. For example, some students are apt to read the newspaper or a book that has no connection to the content of the course during a classroom lecture or discussion. Because this kind of behavior is more overt and visible than, say, doodling on a piece of paper, it can have a more jarring and disruptive affect upon the intellectual climate and morale of a classroom.

I know of two instances when instructors were so incensed by this form of inattentive disruptiveness that they took immediate and, in my view, overly punitive action to deal with it. In one case the instructor began grilling the student about the topic under discussion, knowing full well that the student would draw a complete blank. In another case the instructor actually sidled up to the student's desk, grabbed a book from the student's hands and slammed it down thunderously upon his desk. Because students who visibly read irrelevant material during class are being both disrespectful and potentially disruptive, they should be dealt with affirmatively. I will in a later chapter provide some guidelines for dealing with this form of misconduct.

EATING, DRINKING, GUM CHEWING, SMOKING, CARRYING PAGERS AND BEEPERS, PASSING NOTES

The above-mentioned behaviors are usually disruptive and therefore should be disallowed, if it is the inclination of the instructor to do so. Aside from those who might have a medically based reason for doing so, eating or drinking in class is usually unnecessary and bespeaks a certain disdain for the common decorum of a teaching and learning environment. Gum chewing, if one masticates with some subtlety and self-restraint, might be considered allowable. However, there are students who chew their gum in a manner much like alligators devour their prey and, to make matters worse, they smack and snap their wad of gum quite audibly and uncouthly. This form of gum chewing can and probably should be disallowed.

Smoking in class is prohibited practically everywhere and, as far as I can tell, is rarely a classroom problem these days. If instructors are confronted with a student who decides to light up in class, they know they are dealing with someone who is violating a student code of conduct. Beepers and pagers, by contrast, have become commonplace phenomena in the contemporary college classroom. Because the unheralded and sharp cacaphony of beepers and pagers during an otherwise orderly classroom can be highly disruptive, these devices ordinarily should be barred or temporarily deactivated. Predictably, some students who carry beepers and pagers will argue—often quite persuasively—that their dire personal or professional obligations require that they be immediately reachable, no matter where or when. Ordinarily, however, it is in the decided interest of instructors and their classes that they disabuse beeper-carrying students of the notion that their own personal or professional needs take precedence over the rights and needs of others to teach and learn in a relatively untrammeled academic environment.

The act of passing notes in class is usually unnecessary and inappropriate since these notes, as the note-passing students themselves often acknowledge, usually relate to personal and patently postponable matters. Students who pass notes to classmates—whether they realize it or not—are engaging in a distracting and disrespectful manner. The classroom is not the proper setting for students to be attending to their own personal affairs nor should they be initiating personal contacts with classmates that divert others from attending to the academic tasks at hand. In short, excessive note-passing should be actively discouraged and, if necessary, prohibited.

UNEXCUSED EXITS FROM CLASS

It is a common plaint of college instructors that students make early and unexpected exits from class, often without explanation or apology. Presumably, most of these exits are for the purpose of either going to the bathroom or making a scheduled telephone call. Some students return quickly, others dawdle, and still others do not return until the next class. Is such behavior allowable or acceptable? With the exception of those students who are allowed such accommodations due to a bona fide and documented disability, it is best, I believe, to regard these unexcused exits as disruptive forms of behavior that should be actively discouraged and, if necessary, subject to academic or disciplinary penalties. The specific guidelines for dealing with this problem will be discussed in a subsequent chapter.

VERBAL OR PHYSICAL THREATS, TO STUDENTS OR FACULTY

Unfortunately, reports of verbal and physical threats to faculty and students have dramatically risen in recent years. Some threats are verbal and veiled, such as when an instructor who admonished a student at my college was asked by the student if he understood the term "vendetta." Some verbal threats, however, are far more explicit and minatory, as when an instructor at a Southern college was told by a disgruntled student that he was going to have an "accident." Physical threats usually have a more imminent, volatile, coercive and, of course, dangerous quality. The threatening student may approach his victim menacingly, actually shove or manhandle the individual, or worse, launch a full-fledged physical assault upon the person.

Whether threats are directed at students or faculty, are veiled or explicit, are verbal or physical, are "idle" or definitely malevolent, they all constitute inordinately unacceptable, odious, and potentially punishable forms of disruptive behavior. This principle has received a clear acknowledgement in a California education code that makes a college official's failure to report known physical and verbal threats to individuals a punishable crime.

DISPUTING THE INSTRUCTOR'S AUTHORITY AND EXPERTISE

Certain students, especially those who have received substandard grades or evaluations from their instructors, take the aggressive tack of debunking and devaluing the instructor's judgment, authority, and expertise. The student, disappointed and frustrated with the grade assigned to his paper or exam, may first attempt to negotiate a grade change by pointing out certain mistakes or oversights for which the instructor is allegedly culpable in applying his or her grading standards. When this approach meets with failure, the student may then resort to aiming a more savage broadside at the instructor: a form of character assassination. The instructor is told that he or she lacks the background, scholarly integrity, expertise, or authority to teach and evaluate students. In other words, in the estimation of the student, the instructor should find some other means of employment. In some of the cases in which I have served as a consultant, instructors have been told by students that (based on the students' self-declared superior intellectual and life-experience qualifications) the students themselves would be far better suited to teach the course than the instructors.

To underscore their point, many of these students transmit their castigating reports to departmental chairpersons and college administrators, usually in the hope that some college higher-up will, at the very least, intervene by imposing a favorable grade change on the instructor or, far better, by investigating the instructor's qualifications to teach.

The various forms of misconduct adumbrated in this chapter are not exhaustive. In subsequent chapters we will encounter other forms of behavior that are disruptive, but, as I have discovered from my visits to various colleges, the range of disruptive behaviors appears to be infinite.

Chapter II

Sources of Doubt and Indecision

If the timely reporting of disruptive incidents depended largely on the technical skills required for accurately documenting these events, few instructors would have any difficulty in reporting and resolving disruptive crises. However, failure to document and report incidents that require disciplinary intervention is, in my estimation, usually based primarily upon a complex set of attitudes and emotional responses that often become insurmountable impediments to taking affirmative measures. Before examining those potential measures one might use to deal with disruptive behavior, let us first consider those emotional and attitudinal factors that impede the process of reporting disruptiveness in the classroom.

"BENIGN" INACTION

Some instructors are reticent to identify or address an incident of disruptiveness because they fancifully believe that their inaction and inattention to a disruptive incident will somehow bring about the spontaneous cessation of the disruption. While observing incidents of classroom disruption they decline to intervene because they believe that sooner or later the disruptive perpetrators themselves will see the error of their ways and eventually desist from further disrupting the class.

Often coupled with this misguided faith in the disruptors' desire or capacity to control their own misconduct is another, often quite groundless, belief. Instructors sometimes believe that the disruptive student will appreciate their light-handedness in dealing with the disruption, will interpret the instructors' permissiveness to be a form of kindness and generosity, and therefore will respond, commensurately, with appreciative, cooperative and respectful behavior toward others in the classroom. Admittedly, every now and then this hoped-for scenario does eventuate as a result of an instructor's inaction.

However, according to the many reports I have received regarding seriously disruptive students, quite often the disruptiveness has reached serious proportions precisely because of an instructor's inability or unwillingness to intervene quickly and decisively. How might this seemingly paradoxical situation be explained? Well, it is important to recognize that many highly disruptive students are persons with an overweening sense of self-entitlement and disregard for others. When instructors are lax or permissive toward such students, they are not, as they might fervently hope, viewed by the disruptive student as generous or kindly. Rather, their indecisiveness and inaction are taken as signs of fear, irresoluteness, naivete, or perhaps worse, indifference toward the students' misconduct. If highly disruptive students discern that their instructors are fearful or indifferent when faced with serious misconduct in the classroom, they often take further advantage of their power to disrupt because they construe, quite conveniently, the instructors' inaction to be an implied form of condonation or license for them to continue disrupting the classroom. For this reason, those instructors who rely upon a stance of non-committalism and non-intervention in dealing with disruptive behavior in the classroom are also those who are most likely to, unwittingly, foster a seriously disruptive crisis. Consequently, the term "benign" inaction is a misnomer. Regrettably, the consequences of an instructor's inaction are usually far from benign.

FEARS OF RECEIVING INADEQUATE ADMINISTRATIVE SUPPORT

It is quite common for instructors to have doubts and reservations about the wisdom of reporting disruptive incidents because they fear adverse reactions from the college administrators to whom they are accountable. Unfortunately, such fears are not always irrational or groundless. I have spoken with instructors at many colleges who relate "horror stories" about administrators who consistently refuse to deal affirmatively with disruptive incidents. (Conversely, I have also heard an equal number of doleful tales from college administrators about instructors who fixedly refuse to identify and report cases of disruption.)

When instructors report incidents of disruption to administrators they usually do so, in my opinion, with a certain amount of reluctance, trepidation and discomfort. They are not always certain they are doing the "right" thing and fear they may be called on the carpet for misconstruing or mismanaging a disruptive incident in the classroom. If an administrator responds disrespectfully or dismissively to the fears of the instructor and, to make matters worse, to the gravity of the disruptive crisis itself, the instructor is likely to come away from the consultation feeling ashamed, angry and disempowered. A common mistake made by some administrators is the presumption that the instructor who has been involved in a disruptive incident must have necessarily, perhaps through malice or ineptitude, provoked the disruption. Thus, the instructor may be unfairly and punitively accused of being the actual culprit responsible for the incident.

Another common mistake on the part of some administrators is the tendency to devalue the instructor's assessment of the seriousness of the disruption. This is variously done by being cynical or jocular about the disruptive incident, by pooh-poohing the actual threat posed by the disruptive student, or by simply dismissing the instructors' concerns out of hand and returning them to the classroom to endure yet another round of disruptive abuse. This is not to suggest that administrators must see eye-to-eye with instructors/complainants regarding the nature or potential threat of each case of disruption. It is to suggest that each reported case of disruption should be administratively investigated promptly, thoroughly, and respectfully.

The matter of self-consciousness in reporting incidents of disruption usually becomes particularly problematic for those instructors who are either part-time or non-tenured. These instructors ordinarily have less than solid job security and therefore are especially determined to eschew any action that might jeopardize their prospects for promotion or tenure. I have noticed, for example, that many new hirelings are fearful of reporting incidents of classroom disruption because they believe that their difficulty in handling the situation independently and their resultant need to enlist the assistance of an administrator to resolve the crisis will be viewed by the administrator as emblems of their professional incompetence. Thus, they may isolatedly attempt to tough out a complicated or even dangerous incident of disruption rather than share their fears and concerns with administrative staff. Ironically, and sadly, some neophytic instructors will, by this means, discover that they ultimately have been charged with incompetence *because they failed to report the disruptive incident.* For this reason, it is imperative for administrators to pronounce and publicize their determination to investigate all cases of disruption, quickly and respectfully. Otherwise, instructors will find themselves in a nasty, untenable situation of Catch-22, in which they are penalized for either reporting or failing to report disruptive incidents. This, of course, is a recipe for demoralization and chaos.

There is another reason, one that is partly fiscal and partly political, that causes instructors to be averse to reporting cases of classroom disruption to administrators. Clearly, the *sine qua non* of the university is student enrollment. Enrollment generates revenue and ensures solvency and institutional viability. At colleges where the importance of student enrollment and retention is zealously stressed, one might easily intuit, accurately or not, that the hallowed ethos of the college is to retain all students, at virtually any cost. If this principle is carried too far, it may lead to the dangerous notion that student retention takes precedence over practically all other considerations, including public safety and the peaceable management of the classroom.

At several colleges I visited, where the tuition happened to be pricey, both faculty and students expressed the opinion that some college administrators and instructors were treating disruptive students in an overly permissive manner because there was a general understanding, albeit unstated, unwritten and unofficial, throughout the college that no students should be suspended or expelled, regardless of the gravity of their antisocial behavior. The reason: the expulsion of even a single student would buffet and dislodge the battened-down coffers of the college. If such considerations are truly handcuffing some colleges in their dealings with seriously disruptive students, they should regard themselves as sorry victims of their own ethical compromises as well as dull hostages to undeserving individuals. Moreover, instructors who are being encouraged or pressured to tolerate classroom misconduct in order to prevent the loss of an individual student's tuition are being ethically undermined and compromised as well.

FEAR OF HARMING THE PSYCHOLOGICALLY FRAGILE STUDENT

Quite frequently, faculty reports of students who have been disruptive include references to the students' state of mind and psychological status. Because disruptive behavior is by definition aberrant, an inference is often made that the disruptive student is suffering from some serious form of psychological disorder. Why else, the instructor reasons, would the student display such obviously antisocial behavior? Once instructors have established in their own minds that the disruptive student is also a psychologically disturbed student, a pivotal decision must be made: to discipline or not discipline a person now deemed to be psychologically impaired in some respect.

Many instructors are quite astute in recognizing the signs of psychological distress and even discerning the hallmarks of mental illness in some of their students. Thus, they are often quite correct when they report that some of their disruptive students are also psychologically disturbed. However, once they have convinced themselves of the students' psychological frailty, they often err by assuming that students with a psychological "problem" cannot tolerate or benefit from having their disruptive behavior curbed through the use of discipline. Instead, some instructors maintain that the use of discipline with the psychologically fragile student will only serve to dismantle and destabilize the student, aggravate an already badly inflamed classroom situation and, in the end, result in some ugly denouement. Thus, some disturbed/disturbing students are allowed to continue behaving disruptively with impunity, as if their out-of-control behavior was somehow meeting their psychological and educational needs.

When a student is disruptive and is also psychologically disturbed—e.g., schizophrenic, manic-depressive, borderline—it is well to recognize that this student, *probably more than most students,* requires and deserves direction and limit-setting from others. After all, is it not ironic that an instructor would first correctly establish that a student has a serious psychological impairment and then proceed to allow that selfsame student to behave disruptively and self-destructively in the classroom as if that student had the capacity to exercise sound judgment and genuine self-control?

When students evidence a woeful inability to understand the importance of complying reasonably to the codes of student conduct, it is imperative that instructors use the range of disciplinary options available at the college in order to awaken such students to the disruptive nature of their behavior, **whether or not the students happen to be psychologically disturbed.** Moreover, instructors should recognize that many psychological disorders result in impaired self-awareness, poor reality-testing and judgment, irrational thinking, and behavior that is sometimes well outside the norm. When such students are provided by instructors with well-defined rules and realistic and humane limitations upon their disruptive behavior, they usually respond by marshalling their internal emotional resources and reconstitute by finding some means with which to control and correct their behavior. For this reason, clear and proportional disciplinary interventions are usually far more efficacious in modifying the disruptive behavior of highly disturbed students than counseling and psychotherapy procedures. Keeping this fact in mind, instructors should, if possible, rely primarily upon the available disciplinary sanctions of their college in dealing with all disruptive behavior, whether or not a given disruptive student is also psychologically disturbed.

Instructors will probably find it reassuring to know that a college is not legally prohibited from disciplining seriously disruptive students even when the students' acts of disruption are manifestations of a documented impairment. For example, a schizophrenic student might, while in the throes of an acute psychotic episode, scream at or threaten another individual. This conduct, although not necessarily willful or animated by malice, is nevertheless generally impermissible. The college is, by law, required to extend reasonable accommodations to students with documented impairments. It is not required by law, however, to accommodate highly disruptive behavior, even if that behavior is largely symptomatic of an impairment.

FEAR OF PHYSICAL OR LEGAL REPRISALS

It has been generally recognized, in recent years, that there has been a growing number of college students who have displayed highly aggressive, or even violent, behavior on college campuses throughout the country. A perhaps even larger number of students are apt to level verbal threats of physical harm at instructors for myriad injustices and slights they have allegedly experienced in classrooms. Tragically, there have been cases of physical assault and mayhem on some college campuses, some with lethal consequences. To make matters worse, there are some students who are not loath to carry concealed weapons onto their college campus.

Instructors, like practically everyone else, zealously and wisely strive to avoid dangerous encounters with others. Therefore, when students say and do things that can reasonably be construed as preambles to violence, instructors are likely to experience paralyzing levels of fear accompanied by an enfeeblement of their capacity to take action. Therefore, it is not uncommon for some instructors to swallow direct, explicit threats from students, anguish privately and tacitly and, although professionally derelict for doing so, fail to report the imperiling incident.

The failure of instructors to report volatile and dangerous students is usually not inspired by fear alone. Instructors, under the pressure of incapacitating fear, usually undergo a process of prognostic thinking. They may carefully calculate the potential risks associated with various courses of action. Generally speaking, the choices are usually quite narrow and circumscribed: to report or not report the threat. When instructors opt to withhold information about a threat of harm or violence it is usually because they believe that administrative knowledge of the threat and administrative intervention to deal with the threat will only incite the culprit to wreak revenge in the form of a truly murderous vendetta against the instructor. Thus, the instructor is held hostage by both the terrorizing student and by his or her own mounting fears, usually greatly compounded by having to deal with a menacing situation entirely on one's own.

It is entirely understandable that instructors fear retaliation from students whenever they must deal with the specter of violence. However, it is regrettable that they so often opt to suppress or withhold information in the face of direct threats to their physical well-being. In the process of calculating the degree of risk connected with a particular course of action, they may overlook certain essential dynamics that are inherent to many such incidents. First, many if not most students who target instructors with threats, do so entirely to coerce, disarm, manipulate and exact an academic favor or advantage from them. Usually, their bullying tactics crest long before they will ever actually carry out a threat toward an instructor. Bearing this in mind, instructors must stand firm against the classroom bully and divest this person of his or her capacity to manipulate and intimidate. This is usually most effectively done through an immediate administrative investigation of a threat and, if necessary, the imposition of disciplinary sanctions upon the malefactor.

What about the threatening offender who appears quite prepared to carry out the threat? Should this person be treated with more deference and delicacy? With few exceptions, absolutely not. If a person has leveled a serious physical threat at an instructor and appears intent upon carrying out that threat, that person most assuredly belongs either in a jail or in the closed unit of a psychiatric hospital. There should be no prevarication or delay in dealing with such an individual. If necessary, both the administrative resources of the college and the law enforcement agencies of the off-campus community will collaborate in apprehending and placing in protective custody the person who poses such an imminent threat to others.

Those instructors who temporize rather than act in response to a physical threat because they fear harm at the hands of the aggressor quite often are taking a serious and dangerous risk. It is important in such situations to understand the sadistic motivations and malevolent intentions of persons who threaten others in order to counteract and neutralize their potential for violence. What are some of these motivations and intentions? Certainly, they include wishes to coerce, dominate, overawe, horrify, intimidate, and control their victims. Commonly, their sadistic behavior is driven by intense strivings to overcome feelings of worthlessness, inferiority, and powerlessness.

Taking the psychological makeup of the typical threatening student into account, what ordinarily happens when we ignore the lethal threats of such an individual?

Regrettably, and usually, a pernicious emotional process is set in motion. The threateners feel slighted by being ignored, assume their threats are being taken lightly, and, more importantly, they conclude that *they themselves* are being dismissed, rebuffed, and discarded. Feeling humiliated and emotionally abandoned, their anger intensifies and vengeful desires and fantasies predominate their thoughts.

In the end, they formulate the idea that in order to be taken seriously, they must escalate or enact their threats—raise the ante, so to speak. With relatively few exceptions, this is exactly the scenario that I have retrospectively witnessed whenever I have been consulted about cases that have already involved acts of physical violence perpetrated by students against instructors. In nearly every instance, perpetrators had given forewarning of their own dangerousness in the form of identifiable threats and they were nonetheless allowed to continue their enrollment without being questioned or investigated by college authorities or law enforcement officials.

Why, then, do immediate and decisive responses to threats yield positive results? First, threateners discern that they are being taken seriously. Although they may very well abhor and fulminate against the college officials who confront and set limits upon their offensive (and possibly illegal) behavior, they justifiably realize that they are, at last, being treated with a healthy dose of respect by others, even if it is largely a respect based upon a fear of their potential lethality. When their importance as a person is acknowledged in this way, their feelings of worthlessness are assuaged and, not surprisingly, their behavior often improves as a result. Although this description of an intrinsically complicated process is, of course, a capsulized oversimplification of how to resolve threatful situations, my own consultations with large numbers of instructors regarding students who threaten them suggests that the points highlighted here are valid and important.

There is another reason that a serious administrative or law enforcement investigation tends to quell threatening crises. When threateners discover that it is not only the instructor who knows of their threats, but also others in positions of authority who can take administrative or legal action against them, they are often disabused of their illusion of possessing omnipotent powers to cow and control others. The realistic fear of possibly forfeiting either their educational opportunities or, worse, their personal freedom, awakens them to the necessity for bringing their offensive conduct under control. To be sure, arousing threatening students' fear of punishment in the form of prospectively lost educational privileges and opportunities or a curtailment of their personal freedom often serves as the strongest, if not only, antidote for dealing with this extreme form of misconduct.

When instructors fail to take action to deal with threats out of a fear of legal reprisals from the offending students they are, unfortunately, usually exercising faulty logic and poor calculatory judgment. If a given instructor has had valid grounds for reporting and disciplining students for misconduct, has properly documented the disruptive incident(s), has sufficiently notified students of those college codes that have been violated by the misconduct and, if the college has provided students with adequate opportunities to challenge and contest allegations of their misconduct—in other words, if the instructor and the administrative staff have carefully instituted and adhered to due process procedures—the likelihood of having to deal with a lawsuit, especially a successful lawsuit on the part of the offending student, is greatly diminished.

We, of course, live in a litigious era when certain disgruntled individuals, for the flimsiest of reasons, will sue individuals, agencies, and institutions "at the drop of a hat," primarily for personal gain. There-fore, virtually no individual or institution is entirely immune from being the targeted quarry in a civil or criminal lawsuit. (There are apparently a few exceptions, such as the colleges in Texas, where state legislation has immunized the institutions (but not their employees) of higher education from lawsuits.)

Since practically any college instructor can be sued, almost randomly, by students, it behooves instructors to understand and adhere to due process procedures to ensure that their actions vis-a-vis students are in total conformity to the law. To allow a serious threat to go unreported and uninvestigated is not only naive and irresponsible, but also places the faint-hearted instructor in the position of legal complicity in the event that the threat is ultimately carried out. Thus, instructors who remain mum in the face of an explicit threat, contrary to what they may think, are taking extraordinary legal and personal risks. Furthermore, their cravenness in dealing with a realistic danger is likely to imperil the entire campus community. In short, if instructors truly aspire to escape plunderous lawsuits from students, as well they should, it is imperative that they strictly follow due process procedures, which usually compel recipients of threats to report such incidents to the proper authorities immediately. Ironically, and tragically, the instructor who was killed on my own campus over a decade ago was himself probably guilty of a crime when he apparently violated a state law that mandated the duty of college employees to report menacing threats by students. He also, in my estimation, gravely endangered his students who, with great horror, witnessed the murder in the classroom, by willfully spurning his responsibility to report an earlier threat he had received from the man who ultimately killed him.

In sum, student-initiated lawsuits can not be entirely eliminated, but they can be minimized, and, if necessary, defeated in court, if instructors rely upon the due process procedures of the college, one of which is the duty to report incidents of a threatening nature.

GUILT AS A DETERRENT TO ACTION

Many college instructors, much like most people who do not teach, strongly disrelish the role of disciplinarian. They recognize that discipline, especially admonitory discipline, inflicts psychic pain upon its recipients. Therefore, unless one is an unregenerate sadist, the meting out of discipline by instructors is likely to cause them to squirm and anguish, at least at first. Their discomfort, of course, can be greatly exacerbated by students who will accuse them of unfairness, prejudice, and cruelty. It is very hard for many instructors to withstand such inflammatory accusations from students even when they are patently groundless and opportunistic.

I have often been asked by instructors how they can carry out a disciplinary measure against a particular student and still be liked and respected by that student. I would state my view of this dilemma in the following way: The majority of students who are strongly disciplined by instructors will view the discipline as unfair, unwarranted, and unhelpful. If they don't verbalize such reactions they may act them out in indirect ways, such as through sullen or covertly defiant behavior (e.g., lateness to class). In any event, in the short run it is likely that students will not "like" instructors who impose disciplinary procedures upon their misconduct.

Of course, I have heard many anecdotal reports from instructors whose experience was quite different. They reported that the disciplined students "shaped up," improved their behavior and their academic work, and, moreover, formed a positive relationship with the instructor. I don't doubt or refute the accuracy of such reports, and they are truly heartening, even if only for their exceptionality. I simply believe, based on my many consultations with instructors, that the average student who is disciplined will resent and dislike the instructor who dares challenge their unruly classroom conduct.

Am I suggesting, then, that instructors should go lightly on disruptive students lest they encounter their dislike? Of course not. First, instructors must realize and appreciate that there are far more important issues to be considered when teaching a class than the happiness or likes and dislikes of one individual student. Such issues as the level of academic excellence of the instructor and the students, the level of mutual respect that exists between all participants, including the instructor, and the quality of the academic climate that conduces to intellectual discourse in the classroom, far outweigh in importance the need to please one particular student, especially when that student is a persistent nuisance. As a matter of fact, instructors who defer to disruptive students, in the hope that they will ultimately gain favor with them, should ask themselves why they would want to be liked by someone who is behaviorally obnoxious.

A second issue invariably arises whenever instructors defer to disruptive students. Sometimes without realizing it, their deferential behavior toward the disruptive student will engender in all the other students a deep resentment for the instructor. The instructor is viewed by the non-disruptive students as cowardly, lacking in resolve, integrity, and dignity, and, in the eyes of some students, wholly unqualified to teach in a college. So, by inordinately deferring to the disruptive student, the instructor has incurred the wrath and dislike of most other students. This is hardly a viable classroom environment within which instructors can successfully teach.

In sum, instructors need to find ways to monitor and harness their guilt and their search for appreciation when dealing with disruptive students or such students will tyrannize them and their other students.

MISPERCEIVING THE NATURE OF DISCIPLINE

Many instructors attach very negative connotations to the role and nature of discipline. They associate discipline with harsh, disproportionate and punitive measures and, consequently, believe the use of discipline, in almost any form, will invariably result in cruel and immoral injury to others. They assign few positive qualities to discipline and therefore fail to recognize its corrective or rehabilitative potential in dealing with students who are disruptive.

On more than one occasion, when I have recommended the use of discipline in dealing with a disruptive student, instructors have, in response, angrily insisted that there must be a better, more humane way to deal with disruptiveness than by punishing students, even in moderation. In our exchanges I have always gladly requested their opinions regarding the alternatives they have in mind. They usually offer commonsensical ones such as the use of humor, even-tempered and logical discussion, appealing to the good will and reasoning capabilities of the student, or even taking special interest in disruptive students by extending special accommodations to them such as exploring those factors in the students' personal backgrounds that might contribute to their defiant behavior. Perhaps, they think, if they can establish a palpable link between the students' disruptive behavior and the biographical data the students disclose during their discussions, a referral to a counselor or a psychotherapist might be appropriate and eventually serve as the pivotal corrective experience.

Naturally, I have no particular aversion for these alternatives and readily concede that they do "work" with some students. However, by the time most instructors resort to reporting disruptive students they have already tried most or all of these alternatives and they have, alas, proved abortive. The one intervention they have not tried is the use of discipline, believing this approach to be excessively punitive or potentially counterproductive.

It is essential to recognize that discipline is not *inherently* cruel, immoral or counterproductive. On the contrary, when discipline is proportionate, warranted and applied in a rational and disinterested manner, it is not only humane, but often serves as the only form of intervention that prevents disruptive students from acting toward others in ways that are themselves cruel and immoral.

IVORY TOWER ELITISM

There are some college instructors—relatively few, I think—who believe that disruptive behavior among college students is an anathema, conduct that is so egregious and insufferable that it has no place whatsoever on the college campus. As a result, when these instructors are confronted with seriously disruptive behavior they are often shocked and morally offended. Their first reactions may be to wash their hands of disruptive students by asking administrators to permanently remove them from the classroom without themselves taking the necessary measures to accomplish this feat, such as providing the student with adequate warning and the administration with documentation of the sequential events that prompted their submitting a report.

It seems that few college instructors have been adequately prepared for dealing with disruptive students during the course of their own college education. Chances are, they probably never even heard the term or the subject of the disruptive college student mentioned during the time they were attaining their own degrees. Thus, despite their brilliant academic accomplishments, many college instructors enter college teaching positions more poorly prepared for dealing with disruptive students than grade school teachers, who ordinarily have been taught and advised by their college instructors about how to handle young children who act up in class.

It is essential for some college instructors to overcome the elitist attitude that leads them to regard their dealing with disruptive students to be a wasteful, demeaning, and bastardizing form of activity. If the *fin-de-siecle* college students of the late 19th century had to have their rowdy beer parties, many of the *fin-de-siecle* students of the late 20th century somehow feel compelled to disrupt college classrooms. Therefore, rather than disdainfully shun the responsibility, the contemporary college instructor needs to accept the fact that good teaching includes, not only breadth of knowledge and expertise in one's chosen field, but capabilities to manage and quell disorder in the classroom so that teaching and learning can be maximally achieved.

Coping with Misconduct in the College Classroom

Chapter III

Principles and Strategies

It is perhaps stating the obvious to point out that all college instructors have two essential professional prerogatives. First, they have the prerogative to set academic standards for their students and to grade or evaluate the quality of students' performance according to those standards. Second, they have the prerogative to set behavioral standards for their classes. For example, instructors can discipline students for lateness, excessive chattering in class, verbal threats, sleeping in class, or plagiarism.

I am often asked by faculty to address the issue of how to balance the need for standardizing certain codes of student conduct among all college faculty while allowing individual instructors to have the latitude to establish their own particular set of behavioral expectations for students. Fortunately, it seems that some balance between these two disparate poles is reasonably achievable. For example, it is probably quite reasonable for a college to allow faculty some discretionary authority to determine whether students should be allowed to wear hats in class. Thus, those instructors who have no objection to this particular apparel being worn in class may simply ignore it. However, those instructors who take umbrage with students who wear hats in class would be permitted to prohibit this form of behavior. (Of course, such instructors may encounter some students who will refuse to comply with this requirement and even threaten initiating actions that might lead to administrative intercession or legal measures to redress their grievance.)

By contrast, there are certain forms of behavior that are so extreme, antisocial and offensive that one would expect each and every instructor of the college to take disciplinary measures against them. For example, plagiarism and verbal threats constitute behaviors that are extremely offensive and objectionable and therefore any instructor who neglects to discipline and/or report perpetrators will probably be guilty of a dereliction of professional duty.

THE CODE OF STUDENT CONDUCT

If instructors are unclear about which behaviors are proscribed in their classrooms, they should first consult their college's code of student conduct. The code of student conduct ordinarily can be found in both the college catalogue and in the faculty handbook. There are, apparently, a small number of colleges that have not yet developed a code of student conduct and these schools, in my estimation, are unnecessarily exposing themselves to legal risks by operating without a set of written policies and procedures for dealing with student disruptiveness.

Typically, the college's code of student conduct is quite comprehensive, detailed, and, because it is based upon sound legal principles and precedents, is legally enforceable. The wording of the codes often begins with language like the following: "Students shall be disciplined only for good cause which shall include, but not be limited to, the following categories of misconduct." This preamble is usually followed by such examples of misconduct as plagiarism, forgery, obstruction of teaching and administration, physical or verbal abuse of staff, willful misconduct that results in injury or death to students or staff, theft of property, smoking where it is prohibited, possession of a deadly weapon, continued disruptive behavior, failure to comply with directions of college officials acting in the performance of their duties, and many others too numerous to mention here.

If an instructor, for any reason, finds these codes to be too ambiguous or too irrelevant to suit their own particular needs, they should consult knowledgeable colleagues as well as their chairpersons and designated administrators for assistance regarding how best to interpret and enforce the codes. In my own experience, I have never found a single case of student disruption that was not solidly covered by at least one stricture in the code of student conduct.

It is important for instructors to understand that the code of student conduct is the vital centerpiece for dealing with student misconduct. In effect, it is the "law of the land," at least insofar as student behavioral issues are concerned. It is well to keep in mind, however, that when a particular form of student misconduct is not specifically mentioned in the code of student conduct, this does not mean that the misconduct is allowable. For example, the code of course will not specifically proscribe a student's snoring loudly in class. However, loud snoring in class probably violates the code of student conduct in two respects. It falls, most likely, under the rubric of conduct "that obstructs or disrupts teaching" and "continued disruptive behavior that fails to comply with directions of college officials (instructors) acting in the performance of their duties." In any event, if a student is truly engaging in highly disruptive behavior, instructors should have little difficulty identifying which standards of the code of student conduct are being violated.

FOREWARNING STUDENTS IN THE COURSE SYLLABUS

Unfortunately, many instructors have reasonable behavioral expectations of their students that they do not bother to enunciate or explain to their charges. They may take it for granted that students will not rudely interrupt their lectures, leave the classroom prematurely and without permission, or plagiarize. If they are especially fortunate, a few semesters may pass before they are actually forced to deal with such behavior.

It would probably be very advantageous if, at the outset of each semester, instructors took the time and effort to determine in their own minds which classroom behaviors could reasonably be deemed unacceptable and penalizable. They might, for example, ask themselves: Is repetitive chattering acceptable? Is lateness acceptable and, if not, at what point is an academic or disciplinary penalty warranted? Is plagiarism ever acceptable? If it is never acceptable, what is the correct or proportionate disciplinary response to this infraction? Is it all right for students to eat and drink in class? May students carry electronic devices (e.g., phones, beepers) that interrupt and disrupt classroom activities? Should students be allowed to read a newspaper or sleep in class?

In determining such behavioral standards instructors might wish to share their questions and concerns with colleagues and appropriate administrators in order to ensure that the standards they ultimately formulate and encode are both reasonable and legally enforceable. When this process is finally completed, instructors are usually quite prepared to set down some of their behavioral expectations in the course syllabus.

What is the purpose and value of placing behavioral expectations in the course syllabus? For one thing, many if not most students overlook or disregard the codes of student conduct that are emplaced in the college catalogue. Because they normally consult the catalogue early in each semester primarily to access their prospective courses and do so in the frenetic rush of making many critical academic decisions, they usually have little time or inclination to bother with such mundane matters as reading the code of student conduct; it would hardly seem relevant or vital to their particular needs at the time. Thus, when instructors definitively state in writing those behaviors that are proscribed in their particular classes, their students are likely being apprised of college behavioral codes for the first time.

Placing codes governing classroom behavior in a syllabus serves a second purpose. It accentuates or underscores the importance of civil comportment in the classroom. It is an important reminder to students that instructors appreciate and expect respectful classroom behavior and have the prerogatives to intervene and discipline when students behave disrespectfully. It conveys to students that instructors are not only acknowledged authorities in their respective fields, but are also persons who have the institutional and legal right to teach in a climate of consensual respect. Finally, it hopefully communicates to all students that their rights and privileges to learn in the classroom, free from harassment and disruption, will be protected by a duly designated authority of the college: the instructor.

THE PRINCIPLE OF PROPORTIONALITY

Most instructors seem to have a general sense of how to couple disciplinary penalties to infractions. I would suggest, however, that instructors refine their thinking and their disciplinary procedures so that the penalties they impose for infractions are fair, humane, and proportionate. For example, it is not unusual for instructors to penalize some students for tardiness while excusing others, simply because the latter group of students has more inventively conjured up persuasive pretexts for their lateness. Naturally, some excuses are clearly warranted and credible and therefore should be considered extenuating. However, whenever an instructor imposes two very different penalties upon two or more students who have committed very similar infractions, there is increased likelihood that the instructor can legitimately be accused of engaging in discriminatory conduct toward the student who has received "the short end of the stick."

To minimize the potential for discriminatory conduct, instructors may find it helpful to develop a conceptual hierarchy of prospective penalties to match potential infractions of the student code of conduct. Then, before the inception of each semester, they might review the hierarchy to determine whether it is fair, comprehensive, proportionate, precise, and legally enforceable. To meet these criteria, it is likely that the grosser, graver infractions such as plagiarism, thefts, threats, and assaults will be suitably coupled to such disciplinary measures as recommendations for suspension or expulsion. On the other hand, less serious acts of misconduct, such as lateness or chattering in class, might more suitably meet with simple warnings, at least at first. In any event, instructors will probably discover that an in-place hierarchical system for dealing with a variety of potential infractions will be far more efficacious than relying upon an ad hoc approach that requires them to improvise each and every time they are required to deal with student misconduct.

PROCEDURES FOR REPORTING
DISRUPTIVE INCIDENTS

It has been repeatedly surprising to me to discover the large number of faculty at many colleges who are not yet aware of the proper procedures for reporting incidents of disruption. There are even some instructors who believe that they can unilaterally and permanently "kick" a student out of class if, in their estimation, the infraction so warrants. Such instructors are, usually unwittingly, subjecting themselves to some rather unpleasant legal entanglements. Students are entitled, by law, to the rights and privileges inherent in due process procedures. Ordinarily, this means they are entitled to the following: 1) a verbal (or, in the case of serious infractions, written) warning as to the nature of their infraction, including information as to which code(s) they are infracting, 2) a reasonable opportunity to correct their behavior in order to bring it into proper conformity with the code of student conduct, and 3) the recourse to appeal and contest the instructor's assessment of their conduct as well as the disciplinary measure that has been instituted against them.

Although there is some variability among colleges as to how instructors must report incidents of disruption, most schools utilize a system of reporting that resembles the following: 1) after duly warning the student who is deemed disruptive, the instructor transmits in writing a report to a designated administrator, describing in detail those events and actions that adequately illustrate the student's disruptiveness (it is usually best if this report is routed through the office of the department chairperson, who will perhaps be called upon to intervene at some later point in the proceedings. Some colleges have developed and issued specific forms for this purpose, 2) if the report instigates an administrative investigation, both the student and the instructor may be requested to give further written or verbal testimony, 3) if the initial phase of the investigation does not lead to an acceptable resolution of the crisis, a formal hearing might be convened in which both the student and the instructor will be required to provide further testimony, sometimes with the assistance of witnesses.

At most schools there is a clear delineation of disciplinary authority. Normally, instructors have the right to issue warnings to disruptive students and to report these students to a designated administrator. In California, community college instructors are permitted to remove disruptive students from two consecutive classes without administrative authorization, a measure that often helps to defuse a volatile situation while giving the administration time to investigate the matter. The legislation of most other states does not allow college instructors this prerogative, although, under special circumstances (such as when a disruptive student is presenting a clear and imminent danger to others) an instructor may enjoin a student to leave the classroom immediately, and if he or she refuses to comply, the instructor may enlist the help of campus security personnel to remove the student.

At most colleges, the suspension of disruptive students falls rather exclusively within the jurisdiction of the designated administrator, usually the dean of students. Suspensions vary in length. Their length should be, in my judgment, based upon and correlated to the gravity of the misconduct. In other words, the more serious the infraction, the longer should be the suspension. At the majority of schools, expulsions are mandated through the authority of the board of governors or trustees of the college, usually and largely based upon an administrative recommendation. Obviously, an expulsion, the most serious sanction a college can impose upon a student, is usually meted out when a disruptive student's behavior has been deemed so incorrigible that the student's presence on the campus can no longer be safely tolerated.

DOCUMENTATION

It is important for college instructors to recognize that the documentation of disruptive incidents is not simply a futile, intellectual exercise. Accurate documentation is an integral and indispensable part of the disciplinary process, usually constituting the primary evidentiary basis of an administrative investigation of a disruptive incident. Instructors, like most of humankind, have fallible memories. If they do not maintain a contemporaneous, written account of the disruptive incident that serves as the basis of their complaint, it will later be necessary for them to rely strictly upon their recollections of the episode. With the passage of time, some of these recollections may become blurred and irretrievable, and, consequently, less reliable as evidence. Since some of the administrative investigations of disruptive incidents entail a formal hearing at which the principals will be required to testify, it behooves instructors to fortify themselves with documentation that accurately substantiates their complaints.

Also, instructors should not rule out the possibility that a complicated case of student disruptiveness might eventually land in a judicial courtroom. For example, it is possible that an especially litigious student might file a civil lawsuit against the college and/or the instructor as a kind of legal counterclaim against the allegations of disruptiveness. Or, imagining another plausible scenario, if the student's disruptive behavior has constituted acts of criminality (such as an assault upon or homicidal threats against a college official), it is possible that the college and/or the instructor will decide to prefer criminal charges against the student in a court of law. In either case, testimony that is based upon carefully documented records unquestionably carries greater weight and credibility than testimony that rests upon the quicksand of long-forgotten memories.

There are other important reasons to document disruptive incidents. It is well to keep in mind that many disruptive students are perpetrators of disruption many times throughout their tumultuous college careers. The most serious cases of disruption often involve students who treat practically every college official they encounter with contempt and provocativeness. Unfortunately, some instructors blind themselves to this experiential reality, and inordinately tolerate highly disruptive students, rationalizing and assuaging their sufferance with a bromide: "Oh well, by the end of the semester, I'll be rid of that pest." Instructors who take such a tack are, regrettably, doing a serious disservice to themselves and to the college as a whole. By refusing to report and document a student's disruptive behavior simply because at the end of the semester he or she will no longer be one's charge and headache, conveys the message to all students, including the disruptive one, that the misconduct was somehow inoffensive and unobjectionable; in other words, did not warrant a documented report. No matter what academic course one is officially employed to teach, this particular moral lesson should certainly not be included in one's curriculum.

Whenever an instructor endures or winks at a student's highly disruptive behavior because the date on the calendar indicates that the end of the semester is within close range and the disruptive student will soon no longer be the bane of the instructor's existence, that instructor is engaging in, to use a slangy term, "buck passing." Because highly disruptive students tend to be tenaciously disruptive wherever they happen to go, the disruptive student whose behavior has gone unreported and undocumented will most likely feel emboldened to persist in acts of misconduct elsewhere. By this means, unwary instructors inherit the misconduct of disruptive students formerly encountered by their colleagues who, by dint of their failure to document disruptive incidents, have been derelict in carrying out their professional responsibilities.

How can documentation serve the best interests of the college? When an instructor documents the disruptive behavior of a student, the report usually wends its way to a designated administrator, usually the dean of students. If, each time that same student engages in misconduct, he or she is duly reported with the benefit of detailed documentation, the student will eventually generate a cumulative documented history of disruptive behavior that will be reposited with the dean. Obviously, a lengthy history of multiple infractions of the code of student conduct is far more serious and punishable than a single instance of misconduct. Therefore, conscientious documentation of seriously disruptive incidents by each and every instructor will enable the designated administrator to more affirmatively deal with multiple offenders by referring to their cumulative history of misconduct, rather than having to treat each report as if it necessarily represented a first-time (and relatively inconsequential) incident of disruptiveness. Looked at from this standpoint, instructors can see that they are indeed providing a vital service to the college when they document and report disruptive students, even if their own report does not necessarily yield an immediate resolution to their particular classroom crisis.

What are the major ingredients of good documentation? First, the report should be specific, accurate, concrete, and as concise as possible. It should also be devoid of irrelevancies, focusing especially upon the observable disruptive behavior of the student. It is usually best that the report be free of psychological jargon as well as speculations regarding the putative psychological state, diagnosis, or condition of the student. Instructors are not expected to be diagnosticians, and references to an alleged mental illness or psychological condition of the student will likely boomerang during an investigation if the instructor is later questioned about the professional training and expertise that gives him or her the proper authority to diagnose students psychiatrically. Recall, although instructors do not have a legitimate right to psychologically diagnose students on official reports dealing with student misconduct, they most certainly have the clear right to establish reasonable standards of behavior in their classrooms, and when these standards are not met by disruptive students, they should forcefully state their reasons for objecting to the disruptive behavior.

It is probably best to identify in the report as precisely as possible those codes of student conduct that have allegedly been violated by the student. For example, if the student has leveled an epithet at the instructor, the instructor might place in the report a reference to the code that prohibits verbal abuse. Or, if the student was observed stealing a book in the classroom, the instructor would then allude to that specific code which prohibits theft. The report, of course, should be legible, reasonably well organized, and dated. The instructor should retain copies of all transmitted reports. Finally, if instructors favor one particular administrative intervention over another, they should say so in the report. For example, they might submit the report with a comment that informs the administrator that a certain disruptive student is causing concern and the report is merely being transmitted to alert the administrator to the possible need for intervention at some unspecified point in the future. Or, the instructor, completely at a loss as to how to control, single-handedly, the misconduct of the disruptive student, might request the administrator to intervene immediately by suspending the student from the class.

It is not realistic, of course, to expect that the administrator will automatically grant and ratify one's request for a particular intervention, such as the immediate suspension of the student. Nevertheless, explicitly stating one's druthers in the report will remove some of the guesswork from the investigation and may provide the administrator with helpful direction in choosing a proper course of administrative action.

There are times when the absence of documentation deters or undermines an administrative investigation. The following scenario is not uncommon on many campuses. The instructor appeals to an administrator for assistance with a disruptive student. The administrator, eager to assist, requests from the instructor written documentation of the disruptive behavior of the student. The instructor apologetically admits that no documentation has been carried out. The administrator, feeling hamstrung by the lack of available documentation, laments that no administrative action can be taken in the absence of written documentation. The instructor is returned to the classroom with the advice that the disruptive behavior be kept under close surveillance and documented. When the documentation seems sufficiently compelling, the instructor may re-petition the administrator for intervention. The instructor is dismayed by the prospect of having to be continually revictimized by the disruptive student, and feels betrayed by the "uncooperative" administrator.

Are the snags and delays described in this scenario entirely unavoidable? Of course not. In the absence of contemporaneous documentation, an administrator may impose an **interim suspension,** a perfectly legal intervention that temporarily serves to disentangle the instructor and the allegedly disruptive student from one another, and allows sufficient time for a thorough administrative investigation. The **interim suspension,** in most states, maximally spans about 10-15 workdays. It is a neutral procedure in the sense that it does not imply or connote that the student is indeed culpable of acts of misconduct. Rather, it recognizes that the student and the instructor are unable to resolve their mutual crisis on a bilateral basis and need to be separated from one another in order to quell the crisis and allow the administration time to investigate, gather information, and make a judicious recommendation.

During the period of the **interim suspension,** the administrator may advise the instructor, as a kind of postventional procedure, to garner documentation on a retroactive basis. In other words, the instructor, who, at first, was remiss by not documenting the student's disruptive behavior, may now undertake documentation based upon his or her recollections of the disruptive behavior. Although retroactive documentation may not achieve the level of accuracy and veracity that ordinarily accompanies a contemporaneous record, it is nonetheless a valid report that may be used by administrators in evaluating a student's conduct. Incidentally, in at least one state, the State of Washington, an **interim suspension** may be imposed only if it meets a standard that requires that the student's disruptive behavior constitutes some form of risk or danger to others. Therefore, before an administrator institutes an **interim suspension,** it is important for him or her to consult state legislation related to the legal parameters of this particular intervention.

One further caveat is in order with respect to the matter of **interim suspensions.** Students who are excluded from class due to an **interim suspension** are placed, without question, in a disadvantageous position vis-à-vis their classmates for the duration of the suspension. They cannot listen to or take notes of lectures, participate in classroom discussions, take quizzes or examinations, and perhaps will not be apprised of homework assignments. In this sense, the **interim suspension** is far from being a neutral procedure. For students who are ultimately adjudged innocent of charges of misconduct, it would a grievous injustice to have them suffer such adverse consequences for no good reason. Therefore, instructors should take the necessary steps to ensure that students who have been suspended on an interim basis receive comprehensive lecture notes, are provided with opportunities to take quizzes and examinations, and are apprised of all homework assignments. Failure to do so could likely result in a reprehensible case of double jeopardy.

GRADUATED DISCIPLINARY MEASURES

It is helpful to view the disciplinary process as a progressive one that enables college instructors to use mild or moderate disciplinary sanctions for minor infractions of the codes of student conduct and more severe sanctions for more serious violations. Ordinarily, if an infraction is rather minor, such as first-time classroom chattering among a small group of students, it is appropriate for an instructor to discipline this behavior with a **spoken warning.** If the behavior is repeated, spoken warnings may also be repeated, but the instructor needs to establish a definable threshold of tolerance for such disruptive behavior in order to determine at which point the spoken warning is replaced with a **written warning** (possibly, with a copy to the designated administrator). The instructor may document even minor forms of disruption either in an internal log or in a written transmission to the chairperson and/or designated administrator.

If the earlier warnings of the instructor are flouted by the disruptive student(s), it may be necessary to issue a **reprimand.** A reprimand is a formal written notice that the continued violation of a rule or code has resulted in disciplinary action. Normally, a copy of the reprimand is sent to the student, the chairperson, and the designated administrator. The disciplinary action referred to in the reprimand may include: specific requirements that students must fulfill in order to continue to participate in class, placement of the written reprimand in the student's file, restrictions on the student's participation in class, or a conference with the dean of students.

In the state of California, if a reprimand is ineffectual in dealing with a student's disruptive behavior, the instructor may **remove** the student from the class for up to two meetings. Although the instructor may use this disciplinary measure without administrative authorization, it can only be used with good cause. In other words, the misconduct must be of a seriously uncontrollable or exigent nature and the instructor is confident that this form of discipline is not being used arbitrarily or capriciously. Usually, when students have been **removed** from two consecutive classes they may be permitted to return to the subsequent one without further discipline. However, there can be conditions attached to the students' return to class. Such conditions could include further restrictions upon the students' participation in class in the event that the disruptive behavior is repeated and a requirement to meet with the dean of students before being allowed to re-enter the class. Instructors who teach in states other than California may wish to consult their administrative staff to determine whether the disciplinary measure of **removal** is legally allowable. If it is not, I would suggest that it would be in the interest of instructors to lobby for the legalization of this procedure since it is a most handy and expeditious means of defusing disruptive crises.

As mentioned earlier, in a graduated system of disciplinary sanctions, a **suspension** is likely to follow a removal if the removal has proved abortive in stanching the disruptive misconduct. A **suspension** is an administrative action that ordinarily takes place when all other efforts at progressive discipline have failed or when the severity of the misconduct warrants immediate action. **Suspensions** may include: removal from class for the remainder of the semester or removal from all classes and activities of the college for one or more terms. In other words, a **suspension** can legally and entirely ban a student from the campus for the duration specified by this disciplinary measure. Students who are **suspended** should receive in writing the college's intent to suspend, an outline of the specific reasons for the suspension, notification of the student's right to a hearing, and the date and time of the suspension hearing. It is usually the dean of students who is responsible for drafting this documentation.

The procedures for effecting an **expulsion** are usually quite similar to those that are used in cases of **suspension.** However, as indicated earlier, **expulsions** usually must be approved by the college's governing board. **Expulsions** are usually longer in duration than **suspensions** and it is even possible, in cases involving flagrant or highly dangerous misconduct, for an **expulsion** to be permanent.

Although a graduated system of disciplinary sanctions provides helpful guideposts for dealing with disruptive behavior, instructors should be mindful of the fact that a lockstep adherence to such a system of discipline is neither necessary nor desirable at all times. For example, in very serious cases of misconduct, such as an assault or a threat of bodily harm or homicide, it simply makes little sense for an instructor to reprimand or warn a student about the misconduct. Since the behavior manifested is demonstrably extreme and dangerous, the instructor should not temporize before reporting the incident to the designated administrator, accompanied by a request that the administrator intervene and investigate the matter immediately. In general, I might add, it is sound practice to leapfrog past the steps of warning and reprimand whenever the disruptive misconduct is of a grave or imperiling nature by filing an immediate report to the designated administrator.

ACTS OF CRIMINALITY AND SLANDER

There are many forms of disruptive misconduct that not only violate the codes of student conduct, but also violate municipal, state, and federal statutes. For example, the theft of a college computer, the assault upon or stalking of an instructor, the threat of homicide, trafficking in illegal drugs, and the defacement of college property, are all crimes as defined by the law. Therefore, whenever a student engages in a form of misconduct that can be reasonably construed as illegal, it is important for instructors and administrators to consider reporting such incidents to law enforcement agencies without delay. Depending upon the nature and locus of the crime, law enforcement agencies can be slower or quicker as well as harsher or more lenient than the college in administering justice. Nevertheless, it is irresponsible and potentially dangerous for college officials to protect students from prosecution for serious crimes they have committed on campus simply because they are students. Clearly, the college is not a sanctuary where lawbreakers can seek and receive immunity from prosecution; therefore, any college official who provides such quixotic immunization to a student becomes, indefeasibly, a moral confederate of the wrongdoer and, moreover, may eventually even be charged with complicity in a crime he or she has failed to report.

Instructors would do well to remind themselves that they are not only employees of a college, but are also citizens of a state and country, with all the rights, privileges, and responsibilities that are normally attendant to the status of citizenship. Keeping this thought in mind, an instructor may more easily realize that, when confronted with a student's **criminal** misconduct, one has, like any other citizen of this country, the right to report crimes to law enforcement agencies. Therefore, if a student is threatening or menacing an instructor, the instructor not only has the right to report the student to a designated administrator, but also has recourse to report that student to the police. If the level of menace is truly endangering either the personal safety of the instructor or obstructing the instructor's ability to carry out his or her professional duties, the instructor may wish to have the police intervene with a legal restraining order that would serve the purpose of keeping the student at a safe distance from the instructor. Alternatively, the request for a restraining order may be initiated by the college; this is often preferable, since the weighty presence of the institution behind the restraining order may better serve to constrain the student's cantankerousness.

If, however, such measures as restraining orders have not sufficiently harnessed the student's criminal misconduct, the instructor and/or the college must be prepared to file criminal charges against the student. This could, of course, result in the student's arrest and prosecution, thus possibly requiring the instructor and other college officials to testify at a legal hearing or trial. As indicated earlier, this is one of the reasons it is essential for instructors and administrators to maintain accurate documentation throughout the period of the disruptive crisis.

Over the years, instructors have called to my attention cases involving students whose behavior, while not exactly criminal in nature, surely undermines the instructor's psychological well-being and, by doing so, eviscerates his or her ability to teach and earn a livelihood. The behavior of the disruptive students, in these cases, is often exemplified by their publicly assailing the professional qualifications of the instructor and, to make matters worse, gossiping and bruiting malicious rumors about the instructor (some of a highly personal nature) to classmates and to anyone else with a receptive ear. Often, such students seem to derive sadistic gratification from the anguish they cause instructors and therefore the instructors' growing enfeeblement under their barrage only serves to fuel their sadistic instincts.

What can be done about this venomous form of misconduct? Well, some of this misconduct may be specifically prohibited by the codes of student conduct subsumed under the categories that deal with *verbal abuse* and the *obstruction and disruption of classes*. However, in my experience it is a very complicated, protracted, and arduous process to develop a strong case against a student who engages in malicious gossip or slander about an instructor. For one thing, since most of this particular behavior is manifested rather clandestinely, it is often not very detectable or provable. Also, it is usually very difficult to marshal the testimonies of credible, supportive witnesses to authenticate these malicious acts since most students are very tight-lipped when it comes to the matter of incriminating their peers. Finally, the constitutional protections of free speech may serve as a mighty counterweight to instructors' efforts to squelch even the vilest lies and calumnies a student has aimed at their character and professional reputation.

What, then, can be done if the disciplinary authority of the college is unable to neutralize the misconduct of a slandering student? Perhaps a great deal and I have so informed many instructors. If instructors have substantive and verifiable information that a particular student is maliciously attempting to damage their reputation and their very careers, it is possible for them to consider filing a civil action against the culprit for slander. Perhaps, before actually incurring the costs of retaining an attorney and filing a civil lawsuit, it would be best to inform the transgressive student, directly or indirectly, of one's intentions to sue for libel if the misconduct continues. In my judgment, this warning, if issued with the full intention to carry out the legal threat if necessary, will often serve as a complete remedy. If it does not, the instructor may then wish to retain an attorney for the purpose of filing a civil action. In any case, it is unquestionably advisable to have an initial consultation with a trusted attorney before taking any of the steps outlined in this discussion.

Finally, on the matter of dealing with libelous students, it is perhaps well to bear in mind that many of the students who engage in this form of misconduct do so in explosive and frightening spurts, but tend to wear out and in time move on to target others with their venom. Also, many of these students, although they can be strident and for a time evoke the heightened attention of large numbers of people, sooner or later are generally recognized as malicious and fraudulent troublemakers, lose their public credibility, and are even shunned by many of their peers who prefer to have little truck with chronic malcontents. However, when some students, for unknown reasons, passionately fixate their vindictiveness upon particular instructors with an implacable tenacity and steadfastness, it makes little sense, in my opinion, for the victim of this torment simply to wait until the perpetrator tires, becomes bored with the vendetta, or finds another scapegoat. Most assuredly, this kind of waiting game can be very lengthy, unendurably torturous, and, in the end, highly damaging to the emotional welfare of the victim. It is in instances of this kind that I would recommend that instructors, with the help of an administrator and/or an attorney (the college attorney or, if they prefer, their personal attorney), assume a proactive stance toward the transgressive students by letting them know that their misconduct is being seriously evaluated to determine whether their libelous behavior is actionable and therefore sufficient grounds for punitive damages in a civil lawsuit. If the threat of a lawsuit does not serve as a satisfactory corrective to the perpetrator's misconduct, it, regrettably, may be necessary to proceed by carrying out the threat.

EXTENUATING CIRCUMSTANCES

There are many times when commonsense and simple humanity dictate that one not use discipline even when the nature of a student's misconduct would ordinarily warrant disciplinary measures. To use a hypothetical example, let us consider the case of a student who one day explodes, without provocation, in a long, irrational, and angry tirade against the instructor and his classmates. His language is abusive, his tone quite intimidating, and, when warned about his misconduct, he is recalcitrant and unapproachable. The instructor, for understandable reasons, considers reporting this student to the designated administrator accompanied by a request that the student be suspended, at least until he simmers down. Is this always the best way to handle such a disruptive incident? Not necessarily.

There are several factors to be considered when evaluating whether a student's misconduct should be extenuated. First, it is of some relevance to know if the student's outburst was the first of its kind. If indeed it was the first time he had ever engaged in any form of misconduct in the classroom, that fact might suggest that his disruptiveness was essentially episodic and not necessarily a prelude to chronic acts of disruption. Therefore, a simple warning might suffice. Additionally, if the student musters the emotional wherewithal to appeal to the instructor for clemency based upon his regret and contrition over his acts of misconduct, that too can be a basis for extenuation. Finally, if, in the course of the instructor's meeting with the student, it comes to light that the student's uproar in the classroom was a response to a traumatic event that he had recently experienced—say, the discovery that a beloved friend was diagnosed with terminal cancer—the rationale for extenuation becomes even more obvious.

The above-described scenario can be dramatically contrasted with one that involves another hypothetical student. This student also disrupts the class with a long, hostile, and abusive harangue directed at the instructor and his classmates. This is the ninth time he has engaged in this form of volatile misconduct. He has received prior warnings and has clearly not heeded them. When the instructor consults with the student in his office, the student is not only impenitent, he actually vows to repeat his disruptive behavior if, in his view, he has good cause. Moreover, he proffers no reasonable explanation or excuse for his misconduct. Given the circumstances of this case, there seems to be little basis for the instructor to grant extenuation and, it would appear, the appropriate course of action would be an immediate petition for administrative intervention.

Instructors commonly find themselves on the horns of an academic dilemma whenever students seek to be exempted from even warranted disciplinary measures. To excuse or not excuse the behavior, that is the question. Instructors often joke about students who are excessively absent because their large flock of grandparents somehow perishes over and over again. Most instructors, it seems, handle the excuses of students on a case-by-case basis, evaluating each excuse according to the gravity of the precipitating circumstances and (as well as one can tell) the authenticity of the student's narrative. The advantage to a case-by-case evaluation is the opportunity it provides the instructor to use discretion, flexibility, and compassion to carry out a humane decision. The disadvantage to a case-by-case evaluation of excuses is the vast opportunity—a veritable Pandora's box, according to many instructors—it provides for manipulation, lying, abuses, and mischief. A great many instructors acknowledge that, when they have granted some of the excuses of students for excessive absences and tardiness, they have been "had." Afterward, they feel hoodwinked and debased by the transparently fraudulent reasons some students have used for their inability to attend class or take scheduled examinations. In the end, some have entirely regretted their willingness to accept any excuses.

Is there a serviceable antidote to this problem? I think there is, but it is one that many instructors might at first find rather unpalatable. Instructors can state at the inception of each semester that they will accept **no** excuses for absences, tardiness, or missed examinations. To underscore their policy, they should restate it in their syllabi. They also should state precisely how many absences are allowable before an academic penalty is imposed, how much tardiness will be tolerated without penalty, and exactly what happens when a student misses quizzes and examinations. By establishing and promulgating a **No Excuses** policy, instructors have of course placed themselves in a rather unambiguous, unchallengeable position (after all, that is the point!). It is possible (likely?) that some students will allege that this academic posture is authoritarian and inhumane. If so, instructors who adopt a **No Excuses** policy will need somehow to steel themselves against these allegations, realizing that this policy has been adopted for sound academic purposes, including the very integrity of the academic process. At the risk of appearing to contradict myself, however, I feel it is necessary to point out that, even when one does choose to adopt a **No Excuses** policy, it is probably, in my judgment, not a good idea to do so in an absolutist fashion. Even when one's policy appears to be unassailable and unbending, there are, of course, always times and ways for instructors to make exceptions in the name and spirit of humanity. Therefore, it is perhaps best to view a **No Excuses** policy as a useful base line from which instructors can most capably negotiate with students who are apt to seek exceptional (and sometimes preposterous) considerations.

DEALING WITH THE DISRUPTIVE, DISABLED STUDENT

There are many instructors who, because they are unclear about the law, become befuddled by students who have documented disabilities and are also highly disruptive. Generally, colleges are legally obligated to provide special accommodations to students with disabilities. Must a college, then, provide special accommodations that allow the disabled student to be disruptive? Of course not. No student, disabled or not, has the legal right to be disruptive. To suggest otherwise, would be a formula for chaos and disaster.

The ordinary accommodations that are extended to students with disabilities may include: auxiliary aids (tape recorders, readers, books on tape); notetaker service; testing accommodations; special supplemental orientation; special supplemental academic counseling; special registration assistance; special tutoring; parking accommodations; assessment of educational functional limitations; assistance filling out forms; assistance in dealing with administrative services; assistance obtaining changes in assignment deadlines, incompletes, and late withdrawals; liaison with faculty to discuss special seating arrangements, extra breaks, and room changes; disability related counseling; and, peer counseling.

It is common for disabled students to seek special accommodations through the disabled students' office of the college. This office can provide invaluable assistance to disabled students by verifying and documenting their disability and by advising instructors with respect to which accommodations are required for each student. If the student prefers, the exact nature of the disability will not be disclosed to instructors. Laws governing confidentiality may limit the information received by instructors to the simple fact that the student has a verifiable disability that warrants certain accommodations.

Must instructors grant each and every request for special accommodations made by disabled students? Obviously not. Some of the accommodations sought by disabled students may be too impracticable and inexecutable to merit serious consideration. For example, let's say a schizophrenic student who is enrolled in an Abnormal Psychology class requests that the instructor omit the word "psychotic" from his lectures because this word is an emotional fillip that frightens and agitates him. Given the context—a course in abnormal psychology—this is a patently unreasonable and ungrantable request. Surely, instructors should not be expected to omit essential information and references during their lectures, certainly to the detriment of other students, simply because a single individual finds them emotionally jarring, even when that individual has a psychiatric disability.

A legal principle that is useful in cases of this kind enables instructors to reject requests for special accommodations that would require sweeping, comprehensive modifications in either their curricula or their pedagogical methodology. An important caveat is in order, however, regarding denials of accommodations: if instructors deny a disabled student a special accommodation, they should be quite certain that they have **good cause** for doing so. If instructors are uncertain about what constituent legal pieces need to be put together to construct the edifice of **good cause** in a given case, they should by all means obtain sound legal advice before finalizing their decision.

If an instructor denies a disabled student a particular accommodation with **good cause** and that student becomes disruptive afterward, the student is subject to the same disciplinary sanctions as are all other students. If, by the same token, a disabled student is granted special accommodations and afterward engages in disruptive behavior, that student, too, is subject to appropriate disciplinary sanctions. In other words, disabled students, like all other students, must reasonably conform to the code of student conduct, *whether they are receiving special accommodations or not.*

Another useful legal principle for instructors to keep in mind when dealing with disruptive, disabled students is the following: the law does **not** expressly prohibit a college from disciplining a student for misconduct, even when that misconduct is directly related to his or her physical or mental disability. How might this legal principle be concretely applied in a classroom situation? To illustrate, let us take the hypothetical situation of a paranoid schizophrenic student who repeatedly stands up in class, screams, and fiercely accuses his classmates of plotting against him. It is highly likely, of course, that this student's bizarre, disruptive behavior is a direct manifestation of his illness. Does this fact necessarily militate against the use of discipline in dealing with this student? No, it does not. Again, an instructor may use disciplinary sanctions in dealing with a disruptive student even if that student's disruptiveness is a symptom of his or her physical or mental disability.

DISCIPLINE OR THERAPY?

It is quite common and natural for instructors to feel fear, uncertainty, and some guilt when faced with a decision about instituting disciplinary sanctions against a disruptive student. Often, the aversion to using discipline is quite powerful and other, more palatable, courses of action are therefore weighed and investigated. Perhaps the most common alternative to discipline that is used by college instructors and administrators is a referral for psychotherapy. There are many reasons why such referrals replace the use of discipline on college campuses. At this juncture I would like to enumerate some of them while providing a skeptical assessment of their overall value and efficacy.

1) The act of replacing discipline with a psychotherapy referral is often based upon the notion that psychotherapy is a kinder, gentler, and more humanitarian method of dealing with a disruptive student than are disciplinary measures. At best, this notion is often quite fanciful and involves some serious misconceptions about the nature of psychotherapy. Psychotherapy, especially when it becomes intensive, is

often an emotionally trying and formidable experience that truly challenges the capacity of clients to tolerate ambiguity, painful memories and feelings, and recurrent doubts about the usefulness and purpose of the entire psychotherapeutic enterprise. Fortunately, many individuals can withstand the rigors of psychotherapy extremely well and, for that reason, derive significant benefit from the experience. There are many other individuals, however, who lack the resiliency, requisite level of trustfulness, patience, and introspective capabilities that would enable them to benefit significantly from a stint of psychotherapy. For this reason, many of these individuals, in realistic deference to their own personal limitations, assiduously eschew psychotherapy.

Well, as one might imagine, many of our most highly disruptive college students are also the very same persons who are extremely averse to undergoing a psychotherapeutic experience. Rather, they desire and quest for opportunities to act out behaviorally rather than discuss, analyze and gain self-awareness about their ungovernable aggressions. For a great many volatile, acting out students, the prospect of maintaining sufficient self-control hour after hour in intimate conversation with a psychotherapist is sheer anathema. Many such students would surely prefer to incur a one-time disciplinary measure, even a rather stringent one, than undergo what they would consider to be the ordeal of participating in psychotherapy. For this reason, instructors might do well to think twice before they convince themselves that psychotherapy or counseling is truly a kinder, gentler, and more humanitarian approach for dealing with highly disruptive students than discipline.

2) The essential purpose of a code of student conduct is to correct, and if necessary, penalize student misconduct. Perhaps implied in the institution of a code of student conduct, admittedly, is the recognition that by remediating their misconduct the college will have taught disruptive students something important about the value of conforming to a standard of respectful interpersonal conduct and, ultimately, such students, based upon the adverse experience of being disciplined, will become more worthy citizens of our society. But, to repeat, the primary purpose of disciplinary sanctions is to improve and correct unacceptable behavior, not rehabilitate character.

With this thought in mind, it is of the utmost importance for instructors to consider what course of action, a disciplinary measure or a referral for psychotherapy or counseling, will most effectively and quickly accomplish the objective of correcting a student's misconduct. Having consulted on hundreds of cases involving highly disruptive students, some of whom were disciplined for their misconduct and others were referred for counseling or psychotherapy without incurring discipline, there is no doubt in my mind that the use of discipline as an antidote for misconduct has many decided advantages. To understand why, we might first return to the subject of psychotherapy, addressing its primary attributes and limitations.

Generally, the major positive attributes of psychotherapy are twofold: to help clients learn about and understand themselves more deeply than they have been able to achieve without professional assistance and to provide clients with a safe, protective, and empathic relationship with a knowledgeable professional that enables them to heal from painful and sometimes traumatic experiences. When psychotherapy clients derive benefit from increased self-awareness and healing, it is presumed with good reason, they will go on to live more fulfilling lives.

Despite some of the things said about therapy over the years by some of its detractors, it is certainly not an inherent attribute of therapy to correct the misconduct of clients or to exercise social control over their behavior. Of course, it is true that many antisocial persons enter psychotherapy dissatisfied with their own offensive mode of relating to others and, in time, find ways to curb or overcome their belligerent tendencies. But, this is their choice and they have come to therapy voluntarily and for this purpose. When college instructors, however, encourage, prod, cajole, or, as sometimes happens, mandate, disruptive students to seek psychotherapy, they usually are doing so with the primary purpose of enlisting the services of the therapist to remedy the student's misconduct. Because this is the obvious underlying purpose of the instructor's effort to refer the student to a psychotherapist, it is likely that certain confounding complications will ensue from such a referral.

First, it is quite possible that the disruptive student will not oblige the instructor by seeing a therapist since the level of coercion and duress connected with such a referral (that is, one based largely on the student's aberrant misconduct) is usually quite high and therefore nurses defiance and non-compliance in the student. Second, if disruptive students do comply with the instructors' referral by seeing a therapist, the therapy is usually conducted somewhere within the penumbra of the instructors' disciplinary authority, which means that the students will perceive the therapist to be primarily an agent of social control rather than someone who is mainly interested in helping and healing. Under such conditions, the therapy is apt to be a sham, two persons abortively pretending to be independent of the disciplinary aura that affects their every interchange.

Instructors who feel reassured by disruptive students who, based upon their referral, agree to seek the services of a psychotherapist, should think twice. Since students know that therapy is, or at least should be, confidential, it is quite possible that the student is lying to the instructor in order to get a disciplinary "monkey" off his back; in other words, misinforms the instructor about his intentions to see a therapist in order to evade an unsavory disciplinary sanction. Or, to consider another plausible scenario, the disruptive student might attend psychotherapy sessions just long enough to convince the instructor that "all is well" and it is therefore best to dispense with disciplinary measures. In any case, because the therapy is confidential, the instructor, despite whatever the student says, will not really know if the student is keeping appointments, or, for that matter, if the student's level of interest and participation in the therapy he or she does receive is possibly on a par with the office door knob's.

To further complicate matters, instructors will often discover that many disruptive students who keep their appointments and make a wholehearted commitment to their psychotherapy nevertheless continue to be disruptive in the classroom. After all, it may take many months or even years for psychotherapy to enable some highly disruptive students to harness their own insubordination. In some extreme cases, no therapy, regardless of length, orientation, or quality, will lead to a successful outcome with respect to modifying the student's misconduct.

As indicated earlier, instructors should not assume that a student who engages in highly disruptive behavior has never before received therapy or is not currently in therapy. Time and time again I have seen disruptive students referred to therapy by administrators and instructors who are not only currently in treatment but have seen their therapists for many years. As previously mentioned, this should not be a revelation since therapy is no panacea for misconduct. Therefore, before referring **any** student to psychotherapy, it behooves instructors to determine first and discreetly whether a student has a current psychotherapist. If there is a psychotherapist currently in the picture, it is probably best to drop the matter rather than risk the possibility of a replacement or duplication of an already useful service to the student.

Why are disciplinary interventions more efficacious in dealing with disruptive students than psychotherapy or counseling?

First, when students are faced with warranted and proportionate disciplinary measures for their misconduct, they are usually quickly awakened to an enormously important aspect of college life. They learn, often at once, that one is accountable to others for his or her actions while on the campus and that failure to heed generally acceptable codes of conduct can result in a forfeiture of educational rewards and benefits. For students who egocentrically believe that they can disregard and trespass upon the rights of others, disciplinary measures stand ready—much like the imposing stop signs or red lights at street intersections—to remind the would-be disruptive student that there are serious adverse consequences that proceed from student misconduct

Students have every reason to apprehend and appreciate the import of disciplinary sanctions. They ordinarily attend college because it is a grand, recognizable vehicle for achieving social and economic mobility, and, if they are serious scholars, they also realize that colleges have the distinctive merit of being one of the few institutions of our society that are genuinely and wholly dedicated to intellectual inquiry and scholarship. Thus, students who are deprived of attending courses due to their own disruptive behavior, are surely undergoing a huge personal sacrifice that may postpone or ultimately doom the attainment of long-cherished goals. Small wonder, then, that well defined and well enforced disciplinary measures generally serve as an effective deterrent to or remedy for student misconduct.

A fair, just, intelligible, and legally enforceable disciplinary system has one other outstanding merit. Unlike psychotherapy, it defines, as precisely as possible, the outer limits of unacceptable behavior. It distinguishes between civil and unacceptable conduct, makes available to students due process procedures that protect their legal rights, and spells out the adverse consequences that one incurs as a result of certain acts of misconduct. All in all, then, a good disciplinary system has the unique, exemplary attribute of being both **understandable** and **assimilable** for almost all students. For this reason, a legally sound, definitive, and just disciplinary system will generally gain the attention, respect, and cooperation of students with disruptive inclinations to a much higher degree than most non-disciplinary approaches.

Finally, whether most college officials would care to concede this point or not, practically all institutions of higher education have some students who simply do not belong on campus. Their behavior and their attitudes towards others are characterized by implacable contempt, self-aggrandizement, and incorrigibility, they flaunt an adversarial and self-entitled air wherever they go on campus and seem to have a personal agenda to make life miserable for everyone they encounter. Moreover, they misappropriate a disproportionate amount of the staff's time with their incessant complaints, grievances, and disruptions. Oftentimes, they engage in exploitative, manipulative, bullying, and even dangerous misconduct in order to gain an illegitimate hegemony over others. Predictably, they are indifferent to the legal authority or moral suasion of college officials and, when advised to curb their waywardness, they remain rigidly ungovernable. If pushed, they threaten harm to others or to file a lawsuit against the instructor and/or the college. In short, they are a prodigious menace to the morale, safety, and general welfare of everyone and therefore should be removed (expelled).

Unquestionably, students who fit this description can be effectively dealt with only by a disciplinary system that can be used to legally remove and ban them from the campus. The ongoing, insidious affect such students have upon others, classmates and instructors alike, clearly calls for stringent disciplinary measures that, in their speed, directness, and overall efficacy, are infinitely and inimitably superior to non-disciplinary interventions.

THE CO-DEPENDENT INSTRUCTOR

The concept of co-dependency has become rather overused and hackneyed in recent years and, therefore, I now employ it with a certain amount of chariness. Generally, it refers to a dynamic that exists in a mutually destructive relationship. A common illustration involves a husband who is abusive, exploitative, addictive, and entirely resistive to personal change. His wife, although mired in misery and despair by her husband's selfish and destructive behavior, remains stoic and loyal to him, forgiving and rationalizing his neglect and abuse. The husband, justifiably convinced that his wife will tolerate his every act of malice and cruelty, is emboldened to mistreat her with even more abandon. Thus, it is understood, from a dynamic standpoint, that the wife's masochistic passivity, although not necessarily a direct cause of her husband's original mistreatment, is unmistakably a catalyst and fortifier of his ongoing abuse. Spouses and partners of abusive persons, who spongelike absorb and abide sadistic behavior, fuel and perpetuate (usually unconsciously and unwittingly) their partners' cruelty and neglect. Usually, they do so out of deep fears of emotional, physical, or economic abandonment.

What is the relevance of the concept of co-dependency to the role of the college instructor? If we give some serious thought to the matter, we can readily recognize the far-reaching relevancy of this concept. Whenever a student engages in serious misconduct in the classroom, the instructor is faced, broadly speaking, with two choices: to act affirmatively or to respond with a stance of do-nothingism. If the instructor responds by doing nothing, an important, cogent, and non-verbal message is sent to the disruptive student (and perhaps all the other students in the class as well), At the very least, that message conveys the fact that the instructor is unable or unwilling to address and quell the disruption. In other words, is ethically tone deaf. Depending upon the particular bent of the disruptive student, he or she might interpret the instructor's noninterventionist posture in several different ways. The instructor might be seen as being incurious about or indifferent to classroom misconduct, however disruptive the behavior might be. Or, the instructor might be viewed as a person who is too fearful and craven to take affirmative measures against the disruptive student. Or, worse, the instructor might be seen as a person who actually condones and favors antisocial behavior. Whichever interpretive twist disruptive students give to the instructor's inaction, in the end they are likely to conclude that their disruptive behavior will not be addressed or punished. Once disruptive students have formed this conclusion, whether it is rational or not, there is every reason to believe that they will use it as a convenient license for further misconduct. Thus, it is in this sense that the passive, noninterventionist instructor who ignores serious student misconduct becomes an unwitting codependent of the disruptive student.

I think it important to mention in this context that all instructors, regardless of which particular courses they may teach, are in positions of moral authority vis-a-vis students. Whether an instructor is aware of it or not, the assignment of an instructorship requires that one, in the course of carrying out his or her professional duties, at once upholds federal, state, and municipal statutes, maintains behavioral standards in the classroom that are consistent with the college code of student conduct, and fulfills the various ethical obligations that are intrinsic to the profession of education. To carry out this broad and sometimes awesome responsibility, instructors must each day make moral decisions involving the conduct of their charges. In other words, they must, whether they like it or not, stand in moral (not moralistic) judgment regarding the appropriateness and permissibility of a wide range of student behaviors. Quite often, then, instructors will find themselves in the position of "teaching" many students the important differences between respectful and disrespectful conduct.

I would venture to guess that most instructors would prefer not to consider themselves the rightful moral judges of their students. Certainly, it is quite enough simply to teach, mentor, and academically evaluate students without having to oversee and judge the appropriateness of their behavior. Yet, it is an important fact of college life that gifted instructors might be teaching courses—any courses—quite brilliantly, and yet, because they are at the same time ignoring serious misconduct in their classes, are also unknowingly "teaching" their students some rather unsavory moral lessons.

I will try to illustrate this point with an example taken from a recent consultation with an instructor from a Midwestern college. The instructor had just listened to my remarks regarding the moral authority and responsibilities of college instructors. He was apparently perturbed by both the tone and the possible implications of my comments and therefore sought clarification from me. He first wanted to know if I had been suggesting a form of morality that was based upon a particular religion or denomination. I assured him that I was not in any sense promulgating religious precepts; nor was I advancing the beliefs of any particular religious institution, denomination, or dogma. I was merely suggesting, instead, that it is incumbent upon college instructors—and all other college personnel, in my view—that they, in fulfillment of their official responsibilities to the college (and themselves), publicly uphold and defend decent, civilized, responsible, and respectful behavior on the college campus.

The instructor went on to respectfully challenge a point I had made in my lecture regarding classroom conduct. He suggested that there were certain times that ostensibly rude behavior was not at all what it appeared to be and, therefore, instructors needed to be cautious before intervening (I agreed with him). To illustrate his point, he proffered the following example. During his lectures one of his students read continually from a book she held in her lap. At the end of one of his lectures the instructor called the student aside and questioned her about her inattentiveness. The student defended her actions by pointing out that she was perfectly capable of simultaneously imbibing both the lecture and the contents of the book she had been reading. To prove her point, she vowed to do well on the examinations. When the instructor discovered that she did indeed do extremely well on the examinations, he no longer concerned himself with the student's reading in class and was satisfied with his own means of resolving the situation. He is convinced that this student, judging from her superior intellect, has a very bright future. He then asked my opinion about this matter.

I told the instructor that it appeared to me that both he and the student had given rather exclusive priority to the student's uncanny ability to learn two disparate sets of information simultaneously while disregarding a serious flaw in the nature of her interpersonal conduct. I indicated that while the student was learning the "all-important" value of digesting lectures and regurgitating them competently on examinations, she was also learning that her rude behavior—reading while others are speaking to you can, I believe, be generally and legitimately considered rude behavior—was unimpeachable. This, I believe, was the unfortunate moral lesson the student must have derived from her experience.

The instructor, by now a bit on the defensive, repeated that this student had remarkable capabilities that would enable her to succeed well in her future endeavors. I, for one, could easily imagine her as a topflight supervisor or manager in a large, successful company. While presiding at meetings, her underlings would seek help from her. She would respond intelligently and helpfully, while reading from a book in her lap. Most everyone would, with good reason, consider her to be brilliant, rude, and weird. Her intellect would be widely admired and celebrated, and her atrociously haughty manners would be despised, as they should.

Chapter IV

Non-Disciplinary Responses to Classroom Misconduct

I am often asked by instructors whether there might be better, more humane, methods for dealing with classroom misconduct than the imposition of discipline. Of course, there are an infinite number of ways to address and sometimes resolve disruptive misconduct without resorting to discipline. However, I think it apt to mention at the outset of this chapter that I find it ironic that most of the instructors who have asked me, in the height of a disruptive crisis, to suggest alternatives to disciplinary measures, have already themselves attempted to use a wide range of creative non-disciplinary measures to quell crises, mostly with very little success. Nevertheless, I will attempt in this chapter to suggest alternatives to discipline in the hope that in the end some of them may preclude the necessity to punish students for their infractions.

All instructors are, or at least should be, familiar with a cornucopia of non-disciplinary approaches to classroom disruptiveness and, sometimes without even realizing it, they use these approaches each and every day with facility and grace. For obvious reasons, non-disciplinary approaches should be explored and tested before an instructor uses the recourse of disciplining a student for acts of disruption. Although I believe non-disciplinary measures are often persuasive and corrective, I will also suggest, as I enumerate some of the possible non-disciplinary approaches to classroom misconduct, the possible pitfalls one might encounter as they are employed.

GOING THE EXTRA MILE

The highly disruptive student is almost by definition someone who is suffering from some form of emotional stress. There are times when disruptive students will constructively use the opportunity to

47

discuss their stress with a sympathetic and comforting helpmate in order to overcome the pressures that seem to catalyze their misconduct. Perhaps in the relaxed privacy of their offices, instructors can carve out some time from their schedules to meet with the disruptive student at a mutually agreeable time to discuss, not only the student's disruptive behavior, but also the student's overall educational objectives and aspirations. This tete-a-tete can allow for a more informal and individualized discussion of the student's needs and concerns than is usually practicable in the classroom setting.

By meeting privately with the student the instructor might be able to convey a deeper interest and concern than had been evident in the classroom. Perhaps their chat will enable the student to share the reasons for the disgruntlement that leads to his or her misconduct. Most likely, these reasons will include some criticisms of the instructor's methods or manner of instruction. Perhaps these criticisms can lead to clarifications or explanations that will assuage the student's insubordinate urges. Perhaps, if the student's criticisms seem valid, the instructor can endeavor to modify those teaching methods or approaches that especially offend. Such a conference, without necessarily being assigned an official agenda of any kind, can be employed to help the instructor and the student to know (and perhaps even like) one another better and, hopefully, reduce the student's fear of the imbalance of authority that exists between them. The instructor may find it appropriate to use this meeting to make genuine and explicit avowals of a desire to assist the student toward higher levels of academic success. In discussing the student's misconduct, the instructor might simply share certain observations of the student's behavior without formulating judgments, interpretations, and conclusions or giving hasty advice. As much as possible this conference should be used for **understanding** the student's dilemma.

Prior to a presentation I had given at a college in the Northwest, a college chancellor described how, during the time he was a teacher, one of his students was a gigantic "pain in the butt." He had reached the point where he could no longer tolerate the student's presence in his class and opted to have him suspended. Just prior to the suspension, however, the instructor learned of certain tragic adversities in the student's homelife. This discovery deepened the depth of his understanding and empathy toward the student. Giving the student one final opportunity to redeem himself, he called him into his office and told him, "Look, one way or another you and I are going to make it together." And they did. This inspiring tale illustrates how an individual instructor's dedication, commitment, and profound belief in the academic redeemability of a student in his charge literally salvaged an academic career. Such stories are the exception, admittedly, but as exemplars they can provide hope and inspiration to other instructors who, during the course of their instructorships, must cope with the "hard-to-reach" student.

Going the extra mile with some disruptive students may have certain serious drawbacks. The disruptive student who is requested to meet with the instructor to discuss classroom misconduct may simply refuse to attend such a meeting, suspecting that it will be used as a kind of academic ambuscade, a further attempt to complicate his or her life. There are some disruptive students who, once having agreed to meet privately with the instructor, will use the meeting to advance their agenda to humiliate, disempower, and libel the instructor.

When one provides a disruptive student with special attention through more informal, extramural contacts there are several possible adverse consequences to which instructors should be alert. The especially self-entitled, disruptive student may interpret this meeting to suggest that the instructor is fearful and wishes to negotiate and compromise academic and behavioral standards. Highly self-entitled students might also view this meeting as the first of many special accommodations that will be extended to their disruptive misconduct, thus drawing encouragement from the meeting to escalate their disruptiveness in the classroom. Such students, after all, view their tyranny over others to be their bounty and their due. The highly opportunistic student with weak psychological boundaries might also be inclined to construe the instructor's special interest in him or her to represent a **personal** interest in developing a **personal** relationship between the two of them. The potential personal and professional risks associated with dealing with students who are apt to form such opportunistic interpretations should be obvious. For all these reasons, instructors who plan to meet with students to discuss their misconduct would do well, I believe, to keep the focus of these meetings largely upon academic matters and, while displaying warmth, kindness, and interest, to also maintain a suitable degree of distance and decorum while dealing with such students.

A SENSE OF HUMOR

Many instructors have informed me over the years that they have been able to prevent or neutralize even very hostile student misconduct by the use of wit and humor. I do not doubt it. I have had the same experience while doing psychotherapy.

One instructor with whom I recently spoke has considerable success by employing a teasing, bantering response to mild misconduct. For example, if students are excessively inattentive or aggressive, he draws a frowning face upon the blackboard. This seems to amuse and disarm the disruptive students while conveying the clear signal that they must desist from further disrupting the class.

Humor has many attributes that facilitate both learning and receptiveness to authority. The instructor who uses humor with discretion and ingenuity is likely to be considered interesting and approachable. If the humor is sometimes self-effacing, this may additionally help to present the instructor in a more realistic and human light, thus attenuating the emotional distance that often exists between students and their teachers.

Humor possesses a very special potential for dissolving a sticky impasse that may develop between an instructor and a contentious student. Since an angry response from an instructor may inflame an already heated confrontation, perhaps a light-hearted quip might serve better to distract and disarm a hostile student. All in all, instructors who intersperse their lectures with clever witticisms and humorous allusions tend to raise the interest of students, reduce the potential for an adversarial classroom environment, and promote a good working alliance between themselves and their students.

The use of humor can be two-edged, however; instructors, therefore, should exercise some care and circumspection with respect to the way in which they banter and joke with students. Humor is generally misguided and counterproductive when it is sarcastic, ridiculing, and humiliating toward others. Certain obscene forms of humor can be downright offensive and reportable. If an instructor's form of humor is glaringly corny or unfunny, he or she may, as a result, draw the disrespect and animosity of students. Humor that is racist, ageist, sexist, or has homophobic overtones should, for obvious reasons, be dispensed with.

Perhaps the greatest risk in using humor with an already disruptive student is the possibility that the student will interpret the instructor's attempt to be lighthearted and funny to mean that the disruptive behavior is not being taken seriously. If the student makes this inference from the joking manner of an instructor, it enhances the possibility that the disruptive behavior will continue or even intensify. Thus, it is important that instructors who use humor to quell a disruptive incident be ready to replace humorous approaches with more sober interventions should humor fail to achieve its desired purpose.

TEACHING INTERESTINGLY

Recently an instructor pointed out to me that, from her perspective, it is ironic and unfair for some instructors to discipline students for such inattentive forms of behavior as sleeping, chattering, and woolgathering in class when those same instructors are teaching in a boring, tedious, and soporific manner. I agreed. Without realizing it, some instructors induce inattentiveness and disruptiveness in their students by teaching without the verve and joy for learning that is so essential to inspiring students in their quest for greater knowledge. To teach boringly and then discipline students for their somnolence is, in my view, simply compounding an academic predicament.

Perhaps the best antidote to all forms of disruptive behavior is for instructors to teach interestingly. There are many ways to captivate the interest of students. Often the sheer breadth of knowledge an instructor acquires and shares with students will capture their interest and attention. Certainly, if instructors teach with a certain passion and zeal for their subject and can impart their intellectual excitement and idealism to students, it is likely to make an important difference in fostering a positive, non-disruptive classroom environment.

Some instructors discover that classes that allow for student participation and verbal inquiry tend to be more interesting for everyone. Instructors can encourage student participation by regularly inviting questions from the class and treating those questions with respect and inquisitiveness. When students submit intelligent and thought-provoking questions or arguments, they can be complimented for making a positive contribution to the discussion. Some instructors find it helpful, following a lecture, to divide their classes into small groups in which students are asked to brainstorm about the subject under discussion and formulate certain conclusions based upon a consensus of the group. Small-group discussions often provide students with opportunities to become more active participants in class and thereby enhance their positive interest and cooperation in carrying out the general goals of the course.

Instructors who are capable of providing individual attention to their students usually have at least moderate success in gaining their attention and cooperation. Some instructors are adept in remembering the names of their students and because they are addressed by name students often feel appreciated and encouraged by the individualized recognition. Instructors who also are able to remember personal tidbits about their students or can refer to their prior intellectual contributions as formulated in written essays or classroom discussions often foster by this means a positive working alliance with their students.

Instructors can further facilitate a positive working alliance with students by making explicit attempts to assist those who are struggling with assignments by offering them extra time and help during their office hours. Office consultations can be used to get to know the student on a more unique basis, identify the student's stumbling blocks to learning, and to provide the student with information and advice that enhances his or her potential for academic success. At the same time instructors will need to respect their own personal and professional limitations and therefore must take precautions to apportion their office hours to individual students realistically so that they still have adequate time to attend to their many other academic responsibilities.

Instructors will teach interestingly if they understand that they have much to learn from students. There are times when all instructors discover, sometimes to their chagrin, that certain students surpass them in their knowledge of and passion for a particular subject. Since instructors may take rightful pride in the knowledge their students acquire and display, it behooves them to celebrate their students' intellectual discoveries and accomplishments, even if they were not originally germinated by the instructor and even if, assuming they are not entirely crackpot, they sometimes are at variance with the instructors' viewpoints. When instructors signal to their students that learning, although often undertaken on a solitary basis, is a shared enterprise between them, they invite the spirit of cooperation and collaboration in students. Obviously, instructors who teach with a jubilant willingness to share in the exciting journey of learning are likely to have respectful allies rather than obdurate foes for students.

Having strongly advocated for interesting teaching, I think it fitting at this juncture to include a glum caveat. It has been my experience to consult about disruptive students with many instructors who over the years have demonstrated professional excellence in every respect. They know their subject quite thoroughly, they teach with elan and a sunny spirit, and they genuinely like and respect their students. They are persons of integrity, grit, and an unimpeachable idealism regarding their professional obligations. Yet, despite (or perhaps because of) their exemplary personal and professional qualities, they are targeted by certain disgruntled students who chronically and grossly disrupt their classes. Often, they don't understand why their good qualities are not appreciated and respected. They reach out to disruptive students with tact and good intentions and encounter a rebuff and an escalation of the misconduct. Some of these instructors become so disillusioned by these kinds of experiences that they blame themselves and feel that they are "losing it" as qualified professional educators. In a few instances they have even considered quitting their jobs and careers because a particularly disruptive student has so beleaguered them.

If an instructor teaches for a substantial number of years in a college, he or she, in my view, is **likely** to encounter at least one such student along the way. As everyone knows, there are irrationally angry, vindictive, and at the risk of sounding moralistic, quite evil persons inhabiting our society and our colleges. Some of these individuals, principally out of envy it seems, target especially qualified instructors with topflight reputations. Their intent, conscious or unconscious, is to sully and undermine the admiration and popularity these instructors enjoy with most students. Because they themselves lack the capacity to gain the respect and admiration of others, they employ a behavioral agenda to discredit, destabilize, and demoralize a well-respected teacher. In some cases, the psychoanalytic concept of transference helps to explain how some of these students have transferred their intense hostilities from the emotionally significant persons of their childhood years onto the parental figure of the instructor.

Whatever the cause of a particular student's vendetta against a qualified instructor, it is important for that instructor to receive assistance—e.g., legal, administrative, or psychological help—in order to withstand and resolve such a crisis. By all means, it is imperative to resist the temptation to quit one's job or career because the student's vile harassment has somehow not yet been addressed and disciplined. Persist! And document. And report, repeatedly and dramatically, if necessary.

In sum, it is perhaps well for college instructors to keep in mind that they will do their best teaching—and have their fewest disruptive incidents—when they have gained a good command of their subject and can impart, not just the information they have amassed over the years, but a genuine knowledge and enthusiasm about their field of study. Instructors will demonstrate a true knowledge of their subject if they, first, come to terms with the fact that knowledge is dynamic and ever-changing. Respect for the ephemerality of knowledge is an excellent point of embarkation for enriching one's understanding of and wisdom about a subject; best accomplished, of course, with zeal and determination. Possessing genuine knowledge of a subject is, again, more than the amassment of facts and data. It also includes the capacity to integrate and assimilate information that may not readily lend itself to obvious conclusions. The ability to test hypotheses and theories, form (sometimes unorthodox) conclusions and share these findings with a sense of awe and intellectual power is perhaps the essence of the art of teaching.

Chapter V

Everything You've Always Wanted to Know About Classroom Misconduct But Were Afraid to Ask Your Dean

The questions that comprise this chapter are not hypothetical. Each had been submitted to me at conferences by instructors teaching at two- and four-year colleges and universities located in various parts of the United States and Canada.

Do I have the right to kick a student out of my class for calling me a jerk or a son of a bitch?

An answer to this question must be qualified in several ways since the law does not always precisely specify how to manage such situations. If, for example, a student calls an instructor a jerk or a son of a bitch but does so in a non-threatening, bantering manner and, moreover, the relationship between the student and the instructor is generally quite positive, it is entirely possible that the use of these words, although perhaps injudicious, will probably not be sufficient grounds for "kicking" the student out of the class. Perhaps the most appropriate response, then, would be for the instructor to mildly admonish the student for the indiscretion, coupling the admonition with a reminder that such epithets are disrespectful and unwelcome in the classroom.

There are, however, times when the use of such language might, arguably, be sufficient grounds for immediately removing the student from the classroom. For example, if the student calls the instructor these names in a highly rancorous, strident, and threatening manner and refuses to calm down when asked to do so, the student's language may then constitute a form of disruptive behavior that prevents the instructor from carrying out his or her professional duties; namely, conducting the class. In this case, it is not just the student's words, but the overall manner in which he couches those words, that is demonstrably obstructing the instructor's freedom to teach. If a student whose use of abusive language is preventing a teacher from teaching and other students from learning, it is probably advisable, if not imperative, that the instructor have the student removed instantly; if necessary, with the assistance of the campus police.

A less ambiguous or arguable situation is one in which a student uses these epithets in such a way as to suggest that they are clear harbingers of violent or dangerous behavior. For example, if the student is screaming "You son of a bitch" at the instructor, is livid and pulsating with fury, and, moreover, is approaching the instructor menacingly, there is no question that the instructor must use his or her prerogative to have that student removed from the classroom without delay. In this instance, the principal consideration is for the safety and welfare of everyone in the classroom. Again, if the student's manner while verbalizing the epithets can be reasonably construed to be a forerunner of dangerous behavior, the instructor has every right and reason to have that student immediately removed.

Essentially, then, in determining how to respond to a student who calls you a jerk or a son of a bitch, I would suggest that you consider the larger context (including the overall manner of the offending student) before acting (assuming you have both the requisite time and the presence of mind to make a proper determination). In any event, it is generally a good rule to quickly remove students from the classroom whose verbal abuse is deemed either a serious obstruction of the educational process or a likely precursor to truly dangerous conduct.

I'm Hispanic. Some of my Hispanic students think I should be more lenient in grading them because we are from the same culture. What do you think?

Many students, regardless of ethnicity, tend to be opportunistic when it comes to grades. Thus, they may tender all sorts of reasons and excuses to instructors in order to have their grades raised. After all, good grades are an inevasible passport to graduation and ultimately to good jobs and an acceptable standard of living, the desiderata of young people practically everywhere.

Nevertheless, students who attempt to trade on their ethnic and cultural commonality with instructors are indeed engaging in crass and transparent opportunism and most likely they themselves know it. Without question, instructors of all cultural backgrounds should do their utmost to resist these manipulative blandishments

The reasons for rejecting appeals based upon ethnic commonality are obvious. First, grades should be based upon the criterion of performance, not some extraneous factors such as the coincidence of culture, color, race, or ethnicity between students and their instructors. Most importantly, however, instructors have ethical obligations to their profession, to their colleges, and to themselves, to uphold the integrity of the educational process. Clearly, any instructor who favors a student with an inflated grade largely or solely on the basis of sharing a cultural or ethnic background with that student is bastardizing the integrity of the educational process. Instructors who engage in such ethically questionable behavior in order to propitiate demanding students would be doing them and everyone else a terrible disservice and, in the end, will have nothing to be proud of.

What should I do if I have reported a disruptive student to the designated administrator and no action has taken place over the course of several weeks? I have begun to feel scared and desperate.

This is a difficult question to answer without having all the facts. There may be quite valid reasons for some long delays. There are some disciplinary cases that, because of their sheer complexity, require intensive and protracted investigation before an administrative ruling can be rendered. As well, the college must occasionally enlist the advice of its attorneys in order to ensure that all administrative responses to instructors' reports are legally sound. Naturally, the college's collaboration with its legal staff will consume more time and delay its reply to your petition for help.

There are times when an administrator's inordinate delay in responding to an instructor's incident report is unnecessary and unconscionable. I myself have directly witnessed, as well as received many reliable reports about, administrators who have shunned or suppressed investigations of disruptive students, obviously stonewalling in the hope that the case will magically go away. Dilatory and obstructionistic behavior of this kind is often inspired by the administrator's fear that if he or she takes affirmative action against the disruptive student there might be legal repercussions that will redound adversely upon the office of the administrator. Thus, a case may deliberately be shrouded in mystery and remain uninvestigated by an administrator in order to prevent it from escalating into public controversy and, worse, giving rise to litigation against the college.

There are times—I myself have seen them—when some administrators have refused to investigate even very volatile and dangerous cases of disruption because faculty have somehow neglected to document their observations in an acceptable manner. As I earlier indicated, this refusal to intervene is unnecessary and may also place the instructor at considerable risk. When documentation is insufficient, an administrator may still impose an immediate interim suspension upon a student who is posing a risk to an instructor while advising the instructor to construct, retroactively if necessary, a cumulative account of the student's history of disruption.

I have been informed by numerous administrators that they find it frustrating to be plied by instructors for information about reported cases while they are undertaking their investigations. Many aspects of these investigations are conducted privately and confidentially and, in order to protect the students' rights, cannot be confided to instructors or anyone else. They resent the fact that some instructors presume that, because a particular disciplinary case is stretched-out, the administrator is not doing his or her job. They fervently hope that instructors would respect their official responsibility to safeguard confidential information about the investigative proceedings.

Despite the fact that administrators are legally enjoined from disclosing many aspects of the disciplinary investigation, there is, in my opinion, much they can do—and often inadvertently fail to do—that can assuage the anguish that many instructors feel while awaiting an administrative decision regarding a highly disruptive student who remains "in their face." For one thing, the administrator can at least periodically inform the instructor of the status of the case. Apprising the instructor of whether the case is at the beginning, middle, or later stages of resolution violates no rule of confidentiality and can at least give the instructor some reassurance regarding how much longer the endurance course must be run with the disruptive student. When the case is finally adjudicated, principal administrative rulings can and should be disclosed to the instructor **if a failure to disclose these rulings would either markedly interfere with the instructor's ability to carry out professional responsibilities or would endanger the personal safety of the instructor and the instructor's students.** For example, if a student has been suspended from the class, it would be preposterous and foolhardy, most likely, to withhold this information from the instructor. After all, if a suspended student, in violation of an administrative ruling, returns to the "scene of the crime"—the classroom—and the instructor does not know of the suspension, the sanction of a suspension becomes unenforceable and therefore patently meaningless.

I have not fully answered the original question. After weighing all the issues, if an instructor is decidedly unsatisfied with an administrator's apathy or inaction toward a petition for intervention, that instructor may, as a citizen with full legal rights, take legal action—civil or criminal—against the student without the assistance of the college administration. I know of several instructors who have successfully enlisted the legal services of their union or have hired a private attorney in order to check the onslaught of constant harassment they have suffered at the hands of predatorily disruptive students. Although this particular recourse might entail a considerable expenditure of time, money, and emotional energy, it might, when all other strategies have failed, turn out to be the best deterrent to further victimization.

I had a disruptive student in my class for the entire semester. He was, unfortunately, not disciplined. I know he will cause other instructors trouble. Should I find out who his next instructors will be and forewarn them?

There are several sound reasons to resist the temptation to forewarn your colleagues about a disruptive student with whom you had former dealings. First, it is entirely possible that the student who was disruptive in your class will somehow be quite genial and tractable with another instructor. Perhaps the particular interpersonal chemistry between them will produce a compatible dyad. One cannot presume, therefore, that even highly disruptive students will behave disruptively with each and every instructor, although of course there seem to be many individuals who aptly fit that description.

Also, if instructors are forewarned about formerly disruptive students, it is possible that this grisly information might alarm them, causing them, perhaps without even realizing it, to be tense and hypervigilant in their interactions with those students. It is not hard to imagine that, under these circumstances, instructors will communicate, at least subliminally, some of their fears and distrust to those students, thus making it even more difficult to form a positive relationship with them. In this respect, the foretelling of trouble has a way of becoming a self-fulfilling prophecy. So, to invert a well-known aphorism, it is possible, in this situation, that to be forewarned is to be "foredisarmed."

There is another important reason to desist from forewarning your colleagues about potentially disruptive students. Although your intentions may be quite meritorious, the act of passing on essentially derogatory information about your former students to other instructors can be construed by these students (and their lawyers) to be libelous and defamatory. Therefore, one must take care not to be loose-tongued with respect to information that can damage a student's reputation or academic standing.

Your question underscores the importance of contemporaneous documentation and reporting when dealing with disruptive students in your classes. Had you documented and reported your experiences with the disruptive student to an administrator at the time of their occurrence, that information would now be part of that student's disciplinary record. Then, if one of your colleagues subsequently encounters misconduct on the part of that student and files an additional report, the student stands in greater jeopardy. In sum, documentation and reporting **while a disruptive student is in your class** is of far greater value (and poses much less legal risk) than are attempts to forewarn colleagues about the student based upon your own prior experience.

I have had students in my classes who have expressed highly suicidal or violent thoughts in their written essays. Is this information confidential and what do you suggest I do about it?

Some students, when asked to set down their thoughts and feelings in written essays, are apt to be deeply personal in their disclosures. It is not unusual, therefore, that some students will use the opportunity to reveal deep pain and to cry out for help. Instructors have shared with me many essays written by students that are suffused with great personal pain and suffering.

To answer the first part of your question, no, the content of these essays is not confidential and therefore may be shared with college officials who are designated to help with such matters (e.g., administrators, college psychotherapists). If, after consulting with an administrator or therapist, it seems advisable to gain a more precise understanding of the student's purpose in revealing such personally sensitive information, it may be advisable for you to meet with the student to acknowledge the plea for help, however veiled it may have been. The instructor should make it clear that the meeting is strictly for the purpose of clarification, commiseration, and, if the student confirms the need for professional help, a referral for psychological services. It is usually highly inappropriate and inadvisable to delve extensively into the student's personal life, regardless of how poignant or spellbinding the biographical facts might be to you.

The reason for limiting your inquiries to ascertaining the purpose of the student's expressing great suffering in the essay is to avoid conflating your role, in the eyes of the student, with that of a therapist. Normally, instructors do not have the time, expertise, or even the prerogative to undertake in-depth investigations into the personal lives of deeply troubled students. To do so, is likely to invite a symbiotic attachment with someone who not only craves inordinate time, support, and attunement from others but may not have the capacity or desire to distinguish the instructor's professional role from that of either a therapist or personal friend. For this reason, the instructor should keep the goal of meeting with the student clearly circumscribed: determining the problem and, if necessary, arranging for a referral.

It should also be borne in mind that some students express quite shocking, graphic, and bizarre thoughts in essays, not for the purpose of expressing pain or seeking help, but for the sadistic purpose of emotionally discombobulating the instructor. Another motive, equally devious in some respects, is the wish to cover up intellectual and academic deficiencies by not fulfilling the designated assignment of the essay, which the student either does not understand or cannot satisfactorily fulfill, and instead camouflaging their deficiencies by filling the pages with horrific, diversionary melodrama. Usually, when instructors meet with these kinds of students they will discover that they are blithely willing to ignore and deny the import of the incendiary remarks they made in their essay and are adamantly averse to seeking help from a therapist. In short, it is satisfaction enough for them to see their instructor in a frazzled state of mind.

When instructors read essays in which students express unambiguous suicidal or homicidal thoughts or intentions, they should immediately bring this matter to the attention of an administrator or a college psychotherapist. It is probably advisable for the college to have these students questioned and evaluated in order to determine the level of their lethality, to themselves and others. If they are indeed a risk to themselves or others, it is in everyone's interest, most likely, to have them placed in a psychiatric facility at once.

There are two students in my class who irk me by chattering constantly. I have warned and reprimanded them, but they persist. Would it be appropriate and legally permissible to physically separate them from one another?

Although this is not one of my favorite interventions for dealing with garrulously disruptive students, I have been informed that many instructors have used this measure with appreciable success. Some instructors feel, however, that this requirement excessively humiliates and infantilizes students, causing them to harbor resentment and hostility toward the instructor that only serves to generate further disharmony in the classroom. In my own opinion, students who engage in disruptive behavior by persistently chattering in class, and, moreover, are impervious to an instructor's admonitions to desist, are already acting in a puerile manner that is humiliating and embarrassing to themselves, even if they are completely unaware of this fact. Therefore, instructors who separate disruptive students from each other should not, if they can help it, bear or share the onus of embarrassment and humiliation because they have been forced to resort to this unpalatable measure with incorrigible students.

To address the second part of the question, the measure of physically separating two demonstrably disruptive students is well within the parameters of the law and is therefore likely to withstand a legal challenge.

Now and then students will obviously be daydreaming or reading the paper while I am lecturing. I am tempted to stop my lecture and confront them with a question about the subject under discussion. This will definitely embarrass them since they won't be able to answer even the simplest question. Is this a good corrective to the problem?

I think not. The purpose of using discipline is to modify behavior in order to bring it into reasonable conformity with the code of student conduct. Its purpose is definitely not to humiliate or embarrass students, even if humiliation could achieve conformity. A far superior approach for dealing with such students, in my view, is to stop the lecture, gain the students' attention, and then inform them in a calm but firm voice that it is inappropriate and rude to read a newspaper during a lecture and that you would appreciate it if they would put the paper away. This approach is straightforward, truthful, authentic, and, if stated in a dignified manner, should have the advantage of evoking the student's respect for you. By deliberately humiliating students for their misconduct we may gain the upper hand, but in the long run we may also irrecoverably alienate them and they will learn nothing but resentment for their instructors through the humiliation they have suffered at their hands.

What are some effective means for detecting and dealing with plagiarism?

Before addressing the issue of detection, it might first be preferable to deal with the matter of prevention. I would suggest the following preventative approach. At the outset of each semester bring up the subject of plagiarism and openly discuss it with your students. Let them know that you fully appreciate the importance of good grades and the pressure that students feel as they strive and compete for high scores on their tests and papers. Then suggest to them that some students, because they so intensely fear a poor grade, will, regrettably, feel the temptation to cheat. These feelings, they might be told, are not necessarily a reflection of a person's basic character, but simply stem from gnawing anxieties to achieve better scores, an improved grade point average, and, ultimately, a passport (the diploma) to a satisfactory career.

At this juncture, the instructor might point out that, although plagiaristic tendencies are quite common, they should, at all costs, be resisted. Why? Simply because the penalties for plagiarism can be quite severe. Depending on the particular philosophy and policies of an educational institution, the penalties for plagiarizing can range from an automatic failing grade in the course to a suspension or expulsion from the college along with the shame and humiliation that often attends such punishment. Therefore, students who are tempted to plagiarize in order to maximize their academic and professional prospects should keep in mind that, if they are detected cheating, their long-range hopes for personal success may be dashed in a trice. In other words, **plagiarism is definitely not worth the risk,** and, therefore, instructors should underscore this point to students.

It is also advisable, I think, for instructors to inform students in their syllabi that written work must be original and that plagiarism by any name as well as ignorance of the penalties for plagiarism will not be tolerated and will result in a failing grade.

As for the matter of detection, there are several fairly telltale indicators of plagiarism, although, admittedly, few are entirely foolproof. For example, if the quality of a student's performance on a given paper is dramatically different and inconsistent with the level of work on previous papers, this disparity may leave a discernible scent of plagiarism. Specifically, if the style of the writing, the profundity or complexity of the intellectual processes, and the general level of scholarship markedly surpass that of any previous compositions written by the student, there is most likely reason to suspect plagiarism.

To test for plagiarism, instructors may require a student to redo the assignment in order to determine if the quality of the composition under suspicion can be reasonably matched in a subsequent essay. Also, since plagiarism on essays and compositions is only doable outside the classroom—that is, out of the eyeshot of a hawkeyed proctor—instructors may wish to require their students to write some of their essays in class. Obviously, an essay written in class has easily traceable authorship and therefore the quality of the student's work can be more objectively evaluated under these conditions.

With respect to penalties for plagiarism, as indicated earlier, an instructor can legitimately fail a student whose work is provably plagiarized. At some educational institutions there may be a policy to suspend or expel students who plagiarize. Thus, an instructor at one of these colleges may be required to report a case of plagiarism to an administrator for further adjudication.

I once had a student in my class who carried a revolver that was visible. It frightened me. Is this permissible?

Although persons who have legal permits issued by governmental agencies can legally own and carry certain registered firearms, colleges have generally forbidden students from possessing weapons while on college property. The weapons that are forbidden may include blackjacks, fire bombs, billy clubs, sand clubs, metal knuckles, any dirk, dagger, firearm (loaded or unloaded) such as a pistol, revolver, rifle, etc., any knife with a long blade, any razor with an unguarded blade, any metal pipe or bar that can be used as a club, or any item, such as a large chain, that can be used to threaten bodily harm. Therefore, any instructor who observes a student in possession of one of these weapons should immediately report that student to an administrator and/or the campus security office.

Students who are reluctant to relinquish a registered weapon because they fear it will not be returned may be assured that it can be placed in safekeeping at the campus security office. Students who refuse to relinquish their weapons under any circumstances should be taken into custody and subject to firm discipline and possibly arrest.

Incidentally, I once visited a campus (in Colorado) where a course in firearm safety was being taught. In this atypical case, students openly brought their firearms to the campus and were not at all in violation of campus regulations. I was energetically assured by the instructor of the course that rigorous precautions were taken to ensure that no student was careless or feather-brained while in possession of a dangerous weapon.

Is it a good idea to use peer pressure in order to cope with a disruptive student? In other words, is it advisable to have other students use their influence to control a disruptive student?

Several instructors have informed me that they have been satisfied with the results of using peer pressure to curb the misconduct of a disruptive student. Apparently, these instructors appeal to their students to set consensual codes of conduct in the classroom and the students then enforce those codes through interpersonal displays of approval or disapproval.

I'm of the opinion that the use of peer pressure to cope with disruptive students is fraught with serious pitfalls and therefore strongly recommend against its general application. First, students have neither legal nor official rights to set or enforce codes of student conduct. These rights and prerogatives are legally and exclusively vested with the employees of the college to exercise judiciously. When instructors delegate to students the right (and power) to set and enforce behavioral standards for themselves or other students, they are essentially conferring upon them a legally and bureaucratically unsanctioned "right." Thus, a disruptive student would have good legal cause for challenging the use of peer pressure to control him or her since it is sanctioned neither by law nor by official institutional codes.

Second, instructors should not assume that, because students have democratically arrived at a consensual means for dealing with a disruptive peer, they will necessarily apply those means in an even-handed, skillful, sensitive, humane, and legally sound manner. It is perfectly possible, I think, that at least one student in such a classroom might attempt to pressure the disruptive student into submission through the use of intimidation, ridicule, punitive ostracism, or even physical coercion. Although, I am not envisioning such a classroom to made up of predatory characters similar to those in Golding's *Lord of the Flies*, tendencies toward sadistic revenge can be inadvertently bred by instructors who rely too heavily upon students to bridle their insubordinate peers.

Finally, although instructors may be able to assess and monitor the process of peer pressure as it unfolds in the classroom, they certainly have only a modicum of control over what transpires between their students outside of the classroom. Consequently, it is possible that a

Coping with Misconduct in the College Classroom

disruptive student who is pressured by peers to conform in the class-room may, unbeknownst to the instructor, wreak emotional or physical revenge upon them in their extramural encounters. Obviously, no well-meaning instructor would want to be the cause of or a party to such a sorry situation.

Is it generally advisable to report a disruptive incident that one has not witnessed firsthand?

Yes. If, for example, you are informed by one of your students that she is being harassed by a classmate, and you have not yourself witnessed the alleged harassment, it is advisable to investigate this complaint. This can be done by meeting privately with the alleged perpetrator in order to uncover and clarify the facts connected with the complaint. If the facts substantiate the complaint, the perpetrator can receive a warning from the instructor. If, on the other hand, the harassment has already reached dire or dangerous proportions, it is probably advisable to report the incident to an administrator. Throughout the investigative process, the instructor should let the complainant know that the complaint is being taken seriously and that the matter will be resolved in an expeditious and responsible manner.

If, in the aftermath of this investigation, the instructor receives additional complaints from the student that she continues to be harassed, the matter should definitely be reported to the designated administrator for further investigation and adjudication.

Disruptive incidents reported to instructors that they themselves have not witnessed firsthand are tantamount to hearsay and hearsay on college campuses, in contrast to the judicial requirements of our country's courtrooms, can be legally used as a basis for investigations and, if substantiated, as grounds for disciplining perpetrators of misconduct

I have had to deal with a persistently disruptive student in my class. When I threatened him with discipline, he countered with a threat that he would go to an administrator and, if necessary, get an attorney to redress his grievances with me. These threats of reprisals frighten me. What should I do?

First, do your utmost not to be cowed and held hostage by such threats. If you have truly followed due process procedures—given verbal and/or written warnings to the student about the misconduct, invoked the code of student conduct, documented and reported your observations accurately, etc.—you should have little realistic cause for concern. Of course, if the administrator assigned to investigate this matter is also intimidated by this litigious student, your task will be made more difficult. In this case, you will probably want to meet with this administrator in order to enunciate (and, if necessary, dramatize) your valid reasons for having disciplined this student.

To repeat, if you have properly followed due process procedures, there should be little reason to worry about disruptive students who threaten administrative or legal reprisals. As I have sometimes only half-jokingly said to some instructors, tell such disruptive students that, if they would like, you would be glad to direct them to the administrator's office or give them a referral to a good attorney.

By all means, **do not retreat from using warranted disciplinary measures simply because a student has alluded to the threat of administrative or legal reprisals.** To do so, is to be held hostage to tyrannical behavior. In the end, you will probably grievously regret such a decision because the disruptive student will recognize that tyrannical threats "work" and therefore can be reused in order to further bully and intimidate you. Thus, when dealing with students who threaten administrative or legal reprisals, I would suggest that you first suppress the butterflies in your stomach and the palpitations of your heart (by playacting, if necessary) in order to calmly tell them that it is their legal right to consult with anyone they wish about this matter without interference. However, you have a job to do and one of your essential responsibilities, you might add, is to prohibit misconduct in the classroom. Therefore, you will stand by your decision to administer a disciplinary procedure against the student, threat or no threat.

In cases of imminent danger, let's say a student who is threatening violence, what is the best way to defuse the danger? Should I send one of the students out as a courier to notify the campus police?

In most situations of this kind it is probably best to immediately dismiss the class and then at once report the incident to the campus police and a designated administrator. Since the personal safety of everyone, including yourself, is being imperiled, there is no point in prolonging the time that all of you remain in the direct path of danger.

A second reason for avoiding the use of a student courier is to protect that courier from later reprisals from the violent student. If the student courier is somehow identified by the violent student as the person principally responsible for certain penalties he or she has incurred as a result of the classroom incident, it is possible that the courier will later become a target for retaliation. For this reason, I think it is unwise and perhaps even additionally dangerous to select a particular student for this unsavory mission. Just disband the class and report the incident right away.

I had a student in my class who suffered from Gilles de la Tourette's, a neurological condition that caused him to bark and curse involuntarily. I knew better than to discipline him for his behavior but it was disruptive. What do you suggest?

I once had considerable success with just such a case. The student had Tourette's, that caused him to emit an occasional involuntary bark in class. No one, including the instructor, understood the behavior to be emblematic of a neurological disorder. Rather, they thought the behavior might be willful and spitefully driven. When the instructor consulted with me, I informed him of my impression that the barking was probably a symptom of Tourette's. I then advised him to meet with the student in order to determine the accuracy of my impression.

I further advised the instructor to ask the student for permission to reveal the nature of his condition to his classmates in order to demystify his unusual behavior. In their meeting the student confirmed the fact that he indeed suffered from Tourette's. When asked for permission to disclose this information to classmates, he enthusiastically volunteered for the assignment. Evidently, he was accustomed to this role since he had been a president of a local chapter of a Tourette's association.

Apparently, the student did a masterful job in explaining to his classmates the causes and effects of Tourette's. The explanation definitely edified and propitiated them. Henceforth, whenever the student emitted a bark in class, it was equanimously ignored and life went on as usual.

This vignette illustrates how the authorized and discreet use of information about a neurological condition that regrettably causes disruption can help to troubleshoot a classroom crisis. Oftentimes, when a form of involuntary disruptive behavior is explained and understood, it perforce is destigmatized and thereafter becomes less frightening and objectionable.

Every so often students I have disciplined argue that they have paid expensive tuition and health fees and are therefore automatically entitled to complete all of their courses. This puts me on the defensive. How would you respond to this contention?

I would begin by realizing that this is a specious, nonsensical, and crassly opportunistic argument. I will illustrate this point with an analogy. Most of us pay taxes, some of which are used to underwrite the salaries of the police officers who patrol our states' highways. If we speed, drive recklessly or under the influence of alcohol, we are subject to citations, fines, and possibly even arrest. If we are pulled over by a police officer for speeding, it might be credible to debate the point of whether we were indeed exceeding the speed limit. However, if we instead argue that the police officer has no right to cite us because we pay his or her salary, we are, I think, asking for trouble. The police officer is authorized to carry out the law and the fact that we help to pay his or her salary does not of course abrogate that authority. On the contrary, taxpayers' dollars are used explicitly for the purpose of authorizing the police to make our streets and highways safe from speeding, reckless, and drunk drivers.

By the same token, students who pay tuition fees are ipso facto subsidizing a wide range of educational services. Among those services are the salaries of instructors. One of the official and essential duties of these instructors is to maintain a reasonable degree of order in the classroom, conducive to a good teaching and learning environment. If one of the instructor's students disrupts that environment, it is clearly the duty and responsibility of the instructor to prohibit that behavior. Failure to do so would be a dereliction of duty. Therefore, students who "pay" the salaries of instructors are thereby authorizing instructors to, among other things, keep, much like our highway patrol officers, classrooms free from those who would endanger the overall welfare of others. Thus, students who adduce the argument that they can behave as they please because they pay teachers' salaries are engaging in a crude form of self-entitlement, casuistry, and, worse, contempt for the rights and needs of others. In one form or another, they may need to be respectfully informed of this fact.

I once visited a private college in the South where the dilemma of coping with the self-entitled student was raised many times both by students and faculty. Students at this college paid a hefty tuition. For the most part, they came, as one might expect, from moneyed backgrounds. Many, apparently, had early on learned something about the power and manipulative uses of income and financial blandishments. The behavior of some of these students, as it was described to me, was exemplified by cavalier notions about one's entitlement to control, traduce, bully, subordinate, and belittle others through the ostentatious display of one's wealthy status.

It was the impression of some of my informants that the college, regrettably, sometimes indulged and colluded with the contemptuous behavior of these students. At first, it was unclear to me whether they considered the college's posture to be the result of administrative cravenness or simply abject resignation. Several informants, however, opined with considerable conviction that the college's reluctance to enforce codes of student conduct was too often animated by economic considerations. In other words, the college was winking at disruptive behavior because to do otherwise might, in the long run, lead to the dismissal of a student who was paying a bountiful tuition. In the view of these informants, the college's laissez-faireism primarily represented a determination to prevent, at all costs, the loss of its largesse (tuition). Given the tone of these comments, I had the distinct impression that these individuals had lost considerable respect for the leadership of their college whom they believed to be hapless models of venality. This case example might, I believe, serve as a useful guidepost to administrators who place in importance dollars above rectitudinous principles in dealing with disruptive students. The price that is likely to be paid will be in the currency of staff and student demoralization, cynicism, and disrespect.

I feel uncomfortable about dealing with students who present problems of poor hygiene and are smelly. After all, this is a highly personal and sensitive matter with many people. What do you suggest?

One of the first times I encountered this problem was when a private patient of mine, who taught at a college in central California, brought it up. She had in one of her classes a man who each day arrived in slovenly and malodorous clothes. The stench that wafted from him was grossly offensive to his classmates who, to the best of their ability, physically estranged themselves from him. The problem became so acute, however, that there seemed to be some danger that some of the students might actually drop the course if matters did not improve. It was at that point that my patient appealed to me for advice.

I suggested to her that she meet with the student privately in her office (preferably with the windows open) in order to discuss the problem. Her first reactions to my suggestion were trepid and reluctant. She feared that her questions about the student's hygiene would severely injure and humiliate him, and that no good could come of that. After all, she pointed out, he probably was not aware of how he was affecting others and, moreover, there were clear indications that he was an emotionally fragile person who might be dismantled by criticisms of his personal hygiene.

In response, I told this instructor that I agreed with her opinion that the student probably was not aware of his affect upon others. As a matter of fact, I added, this was one of the main reasons for talking with the student. If the student was indeed oblivious to his adverse affect upon others, it was the instructor's responsibility to point this out to him. By what better means could he understand how and why his classmates resented and ebbed away from him? One of the main goals of meeting with the student, then, was to **awaken** him to the offensive affect his noisome behavior was having upon others in order for him to take steps to correct it. Commonsense suggests that a student who does not truly know that a certain form of behavior is offensive to others will repeat that behavior indefinitely.

Next, the instructor and I discussed **how** she would encourage the student to take corrective measures for dealing with the problem of hygiene. I suggested that she give the student the benefit of her doubts by letting him know that, although he did not mean to offend others, it was necessary for her to tell him that his hygiene was a source of concern and offense in the classroom and therefore needed to be corrected. Obviously, the tone of such a communication should be non-judgmental, empathic, and supportive. If the student reveals that there are certain environmental impediments to improving his hygiene, such as the absence of bathing facilities at home, the instructor might suggest alternatives, such as the use of the shower facilities at the college. In any event, before concluding this meeting, the instructor should make it clear that the problem of the student's unacceptable hygiene **must** be taken care of by the student.

One further point is in order. By expecting and requiring students to maintain acceptable hygienic standards, instructors are doing no more than reminding them to respect the needs and rights of their college classmates. This, then, is a perfectly estimable expectation and requirement. Furthermore, students who literally clean up their act will, as a result, most likely be regarded with more respect, friendliness, and consideration by their peers. Thus, if they fulfill the requirement to correct their hygiene, they are likely to form better relationships with others. In this respect, the instructor who constructively addresses this issue with a problematic student may in the end—as a kind of bonus—be rewarded with the knowledge of having become the agent of positive social change.

In any case, it is generally essential for instructors to avoid forming the misconception that the problem of the seriously unhygienic student is too frivolous, trivial, or personally intimate to be addressed and corrected, directly and affirmatively.

I teach a chemistry lab course. Some of the chemicals we use in the lab are potentially dangerous to particular students such as, for example, pregnant women. Should I provide verbal and written warnings to these students about the dangerous toxicity of these chemicals?

It is definitely advisable to let your students know the full extent of the medical risks to which they might be exposed in your laboratory. If there are particular chemicals to which certain persons, like pregnant women, might be highly susceptible, your students should know exactly which chemicals pose such a hazard to them. These warnings should be conveyed in written form at the inception of each semester and verbally repeated as helpful reminders from time to time.

By the way, it is quite appropriate for all instructors, regardless of their field of study, to inform their classes at the beginning of each semester that students who have reason to expect that they might experience a medical crisis in the classroom (e.g., an epileptic seizure) may, if they wish, confidentially apprise the instructor of the nature of their medical condition and together formulate a sound strategy for safely resolving a crisis should one eventuate.

You have often discussed the problem of lateness. How late is late?

This is difficult to answer precisely and arbitrarily since the line must be drawn by each instructor according to his or her own sensibilities, standards, and emotional thresholds for such forms of misconduct. I would suggest, however, based upon the recommendations of many colleagues, that students should be considered late if they arrive in class at least ten minutes after the official starting time. There are more stringent instructors of my acquaintance who will brook no lateness whatsoever. Students are late and demerited when they arrive at any time after the official starting time. In some cases instructors will close the door at starting time and have given students prior warning not to come in after the door is closed; in other words, take an absence for being late.

Although there is definite merit, I believe, in using a stringent policy toward lateness, there are of course many instructors who will find it very difficult, for psychological or philosophical reasons, to implement this kind of approach. Fortunately, to accommodate differences in personality and philosophy, colleges usually allow their instructors considerable latitude in setting rules and policies regarding lateness. One suggestion: If you discover that a policy of leniency and flexibility toward lateness is being abused, discard it and replace it with a more exacting one before you are overcome with apoplexy.

There is another issue I would like to mention in relation to the problem of lateness. I have observed that many students who are late to class are entirely unmindful of the simple courtesies that might mitigate their behavior in the eyes of their instructors. For example, it is quite common for students who are late to walk right in front of their lecturing instructors without apologizing with a simple "Excuse me" or "Sorry." At the risk of appearing to be an old-fashioned fuddy-duddy, I would suggest that these moments are golden opportunities to teach students something important about manners and civility. I'd recommend that instructors at the outset of each semester, as they set down rules about lateness, state something like the following to their students: "I'd appreciate it, in the event that you arrive late to class and have interrupted my lecture or a classroom discussion, if you would please apologize by saying "Excuse me" or with some similar comment. Thank you." When students do apologize for their lateness, instructors can repeat their "Thank you" verbally to signal their appreciation for this act of courtesy.

Finally, it is important for instructors to realize that rules about lateness cannot be reasonably enforced unless they themselves adhere to high standards with respect to punctuality and attendance. Reliable reports abound on all campuses about instructors who are regularly and heedlessly tardy. Several years ago, an instructor on my own campus remarked to me how passionately devoted he was to the profession of teaching and how much he enjoyed being in the classroom. When I asked his permission to visit one of his classes in order to do a brief "commercial" about the mental health program, he generously suggested that I drop in, unannounced, at the beginning of any class.

Taking him at his word, I came by the following week at the very beginning of one of his classes. Most of the students had already arrived and were seated. When I asked after their instructor, they smirked and rather sarcastically stated that he, as usual, would be about ten minutes late. I took the liberty to give my spiel about the psychological services and, sure enough, the instructor arrived about ten minutes later. Finding me already well along in talking to his students, he appeared as one who had been caught red-handed, and, blushing and stammering with pained embarrassment, he apologized for his flat-footed tardiness. I have never doubted the avowed passion for teaching of this now-retired instructor, but I also believe his habit of being late to class may have gone some way toward tamping the passion of his students to learn from him.

What do you suggest can be done about the misuse of college computers? Some individuals are violating the rights of others by breaking into their programs.

In this age of cyberspace, there is a considerable amount of mischief that is perpetrated through the misuse of college computers. Some malefactors use computers to send hate mail to others, usually anonymously. By stealing passwords in the computer labs, some students purloin accounts, modify or erase the files of other students or overwhelm the resources of a particular program so that it becomes totally useless to its hapless owner. Some send unsolicited and unauthorized E-mail through the stolen files of other students. The college computer has also become a modern-day appliance with which some students are able to carry out a newfangled form of sexual harassment: retrieving pornography from the Internet, introducing it into a woman's program (usually the victim is a woman) and displaying it on her screen. On my campus, a student in a computer lab deliberately sabotaged the computer system of a large library, shutting it down for an entire day.

Most of the above-mentioned examples of the misemployment of computers are genuine acts of criminality and should be treated accordingly. In other words, whenever an instructor encounters a case of a deliberate misuse of a computer as has been just described, it is probably advisable to report the matter to the campus or city police for the purpose of initiating a legal investigation. A student who has been found guilty of deliberate computer violations by the police or by campus authorities should probably be subject to the penalty of suspension or expulsion. As mentioned earlier, the fact that a person who commits a crime happens to be a student should not provide the culprit with any more legal immunity from prosecution than other citizens.

What is the best way to deal with a student who is demonstrably drunk in the classroom?

Students who are demonstrably drunk are most likely going to be rather incoherent, confused, unsteady on their feet, and will manifest some disruptive behavior such as sleeping in a bedraggled and sprawling manner or shouting uncontrollably. Students, if truly drunk, are of course also likely to give off a telltale whiff of whatever alcoholic beverage has just been imbibed. When dealing with such students, it is usually advisable for instructors to tell them, quietly and unobtrusively, to leave the class at once. If they refuse and are generally uncooperative, call a campus security officer to assist you.

At your earliest convenience, file a report on a drunken student with the designated administrator accompanied by a request for disciplinary intervention. Appearing in class in a drunken state is a serious matter and normally warrants a fairly stiff penalty. When filing this report, stress in your description of the incident the student's **behavior**—e.g., shouting, incoherency of speech, unresponsiveness to your directives, stumbling about the classroom, sleeping, emitting the powerful odor of alcohol, etc.—rather than your assessment of drunkenness. Although you are likely to be correct in your assessment, in a disciplinary hearing it may be difficult for you to substantiate and defend your allegation that the student was indeed drunk because you, after all, had no definite proof of same; that is, you had no way of knowing the exact level of alcohol in the student's bloodstream at the time of the incident. (Perhaps the police, if they afterward tested for blood alcohol level and ascertained inebriation, could assist you by testifying at a hearing.) On the other hand, you have very solid, quite unimpeachable evidence of the student's level of disruptiveness through your direct observations of the overt **behavior.** Therefore, it is this **behavior** that should be documented and reported.

A word of caution is in order. There are times when a medical condition (such as diabetes) or the flare-up of a medication (such as an antihistamine) could cause a student to behave in a manner that simulates drunkenness. Therefore, before presuming drunkenness, it might be well to ask such students a few questions about their overall health and whether they are using a medication before requesting that they leave the classroom. If it appears that they are actually suffering from an adverse physiological reaction, the wisest approach would be to call for immediate medical assistance.

A student of mine recently sent me a love letter. It was entirely unsolicited, unexpected, and unwelcome. It frightens me. What should I do about her?

You have the option, if you wish to use it, to meet with the student to discuss the letter. If you do so, take several precautions. Since the student has already evinced a romantic interest in you, you might find it preferable to meet with the office door open or with witnesses in view in order to remove any taint of impropriety that might be introduced by the student afterward. In discussing the letter with the student, you might tell her that the contents of the letter were, as you have already stated, unsolicited and unwelcome. Without, of course, being brutally rejecting, you probably should state that the confection of love sentiments described in the letter will definitely not be reciprocated and do not at all apply to the essential (strictly academic) nature of your relationship with her. If you feel that the student is heated and headstrong about pursuing a personal relationship with you, it may be necessary to allow a censorious tone to enter your voice along with the warning that you are willing to report the matter to an administrator for disciplinary intervention.

By all means, if you can help it, do not become aflutter or inflated with erotic or narcissistic excitement in response to the student's romantic overture. Keep in mind that instructors are generally bright, interesting and charismatic individuals who can quickly animate the intense hopes and yearnings of young students who are seeking the bond of an idealized relationship with such persons. Although these feelings should be responded to with understanding and empathy, it would probably be entirely inappropriate for the instructor to express pleasure or appreciation to such a student for being so "honored" through a love letter. Instead, it should be pointed out that it is definitely in your mutual interest to entirely confine your communications to matters academic.

If, as some instructors are wont to do in such circumstances, the student is invited to further delve into and express her amorous fantasies about the relationship, there most likely will be an intensification of her romantic attachment to the instructor based upon the interest he has just displayed in her ruminations of love. Naturally, this intensification will be accelerated if the experience of the discussion of love is repeated or if the instructor meets with the student anywhere other than in the academic setting.

As practically everyone knows, instructors who breach the formalized boundaries between themselves and students by forming sexual relationships with them are engaging in a grim game of professional Russian roulette. Students embroiled in a romantic relationship with an instructor may at any time—for example, when at some indefinable moment they believe their love is unrequited—become mean and retaliatory and their behavior toward the instructor can take a pernicious turn. Allegations of sexual harassment are not unusual in such cases. Furthermore, some schools, like Yale University, are, at this writing, adopting policies to prohibit instructors from becoming sexually involved with students under their supervision. Thus, at least at these schools, instructors who do become deeply personally involved with their students may in the process be jeopardizing their professional careers. The playwright David Mamet has brilliantly depicted just such an academic imbroglio in his play *Oleana*.

To return to the original question, if you do not wish to meet with the student about her written communication to you, forward a copy of it to the designated administrator for investigation and resolution. Afterward, consult with the administrator to determine the outcome of the investigation. Of course, if the behavior persists or escalates, repetition the administrator for assistance. If absolutely necessary, you can warn the student that persistent behavior of this kind can constitute the crime of stalking and will be reported for criminal investigation if it continues.

How do you feel about parents bringing their young children or even small babies to class? I find it hard to turn this request down when they play on my heartstrings with stories about the difficulty of finding babysitters or child-care services.

One of the first times I encountered this problem was when, as a guest, I visited a class on one of the campuses of the University of California. The class was being taught in a large lecture hall. A young woman entered the room with a small baby in her arms and proceeded to take a seat in the middle of the room. The instructor gave a highly interesting lecture, enlivening his talk with humorous asides and relevant illustrations. Nevertheless, I, and apparently many of his students, judging from their evident restiveness, found it difficult to concentrate on his lecture. The baby had begun to cry noisily almost from the very beginning of the class and continued on through most of the hour. Apparently very hungry, sick or just plain cranky, it could not be soothed by the mother's offerings of food or coddling.

Somewhat exasperated, I whispered to the student next to me, "Does that student have permission to bring her child to class?" I was told that the instructor had informed the class at the beginning of the semester that he had given permission to the student to bring the child to class. He also let it be known that he did not find it distracting to have a crying child in class. I then queried my "classmate," Well, what about the other students? Don't they object?" I was told that there were an appreciable number of students who had voiced complaints about the baby, albeit *sotto voce*. Apparently no one wanted to express a grievance directly to the instructor for fear of offending him or the child's mother. This, in my view, is a sorry situation.

It is of course extremely regrettable that students with parental responsibilities sometimes cannot find or afford the supportive child-care services they need in order to attend college without bringing their children along with them. However, instructors should be mindful of the strong possibility that a noisy or crying child in a classroom will likely distract many of their students and consequently diminish their comprehension of the contents of lectures. I think it is unfair and thoughtless, therefore, for instructors, like the one whose class I visited, to enter into bilateral agreements with parents to have the latter's children in class with them. I also think it would be heavy-handed and disingenuous for an instructor to survey a given class of students in order to determine whether they favor or disfavor the presence of a child in class. After all, it is not likely that many students would care to go on public record as opposing a parent who appears to be fending desperately for herself and her child without adequate child-care resources.

What, then, should be done about this problem? I would recommend either of two possible courses of action. One, an instructor can simply prohibit parents from bringing their children to class under any circumstance. If instituted, this policy should be spelled out in the syllabus with, if one thinks it is necessary, an explanation and an apology to those who may be inconvenienced by the restriction. Or, an instructor can inform students that they may bring a child to class; however, if that child's presence becomes disruptive for any reason, the parent must remove the child from the classroom at once.

One proviso: Some schools must prohibit the presence of children on school grounds because they pose the risk of legal liablility. Naturally, instructors who teach at those institutions will have no choice but to honor this prohibition.

What do you think of the advisability of video-taping a student who has been disruptive in class in order to acquire visual evidence of misconduct?

Although this evidence-gathering procedure may be legally allowable, it has, in my view, more drawbacks than advantages in its implementation. First, for a video-taping to successfully snare a disruptive student, it will most likely have to be used surreptitiously. After all, disruptive students who discover that a video-tape is being used to entrap them in a classroom are not likely to stage an act of misconduct for the benefit of the instructor. But, as one can easily imagine, instructors who engage in watchdoging their students with hidden cameras, if discovered, will not be viewed with especial trust by most of their students. So, in their zeal to "catch a thief" on film, instructors may also ensnare the animosity of their students.

Second, if a camera is in full view of the students and its purpose is apparent, it is not likely to have much utility. Disruptive students would have to be particularly inane and foolhardy to engage in overt misconduct while being the principal subjects of films that are obviously being used to incriminate them. If anything, they may use the filming as a grand opportunity to dissemble model behavior in order to flummox the instructor.

Finally, even though a film may appear to yield greater verisimilitude than other forms of fact-gathering, it is usually not, as the infamous Rodney King case illustrated, an unassailable font of the Truth. In my opinion, instructors can deal quite effectively with disruptive students if they simply rely upon their own observations and possibly the observations of witnesses to document and report incidents of disruption. The add-on use of cinematographic evidence is, in my view, likely to divert, confound, and ultimately undermine, an investigation of the facts.

What in your view is the best way to intervene with students who chatter in class?

I have encountered this problem quite often as a guest lecturer on my own campus. Naturally, a guest lecturer, much like substitute teachers in high schools, will inspire some students to be inattentive and disrespectful. I have found it helpful whenever I am distracted by chattering students to stop my lecture and address the chatterboxes as soon as possible; that is, before my blood becomes aboil and I cannot concentrate on what I am saying. In polite, quiet but firm tones I ask the students to stop talking because I find it distracting. If, after they have received this admonition, they continue to chatter, I might again stop my lecture and this time say, "I'd appreciate it if you would stop talking with one another. It is disruptive. However, if you can't, then I think you ought to leave the class. Which would you prefer?"

In the vast majority of such instances, the students not only ceased talking when confronted with this choice, but actually took reparative steps to atone and overcome their embarrassment by constructively participating in the class discussion that took place afterward. However, if students do not stop chattering and they do not leave the classroom when given this choice, they should be given a written warning by the instructor at the end of the class informing them that they have just violated a code of student conduct and that continued misconduct on their part will be reported to an administrator for the purpose of invoking discipline. By the way, this first written warning can be transmitted to the designated administrator in order to set the groundwork for possible future investigations of misconduct.

Let's say there is a large clique of students who are engaging in chattering. How do you know where to begin? Isn't it unfair to target just one of two of the group with warnings?

I don't think so. An instructor should not be expected to perform with Sherlock Holmesesque precision and perspicacity in deducing exactly which students should principally be held responsible for the disruption caused by a clique. If it is possible to discern that one or two of the students in the group are spearheading the disruption, then of course these students in particular might be given warnings. However, if the disruption has murkier origins, then it might be entirely appropriate to arbitrarily select one or two students for written warnings. If the response to a written warning is "Why me?", the student can be told: "You are being selected for this distinction because you were definitely one of the disruptive students. I am not a detective and will not waste time trying to figure out who is the main culprit here. If you don't want to be disciplined, I would suggest that you either get out of that clique or find some way to control your own conduct when you are with them."

If this measure—designating one or two students as examples by disciplining their disruptive behavior—is not particularly successful, then the instructor may have to consider going through the entire clique, disciplining one student after the other—in the manner, to use an unfortunate analogy, of knocking over stacked bowling pins—until the collective disruption is finally quelled. Not a very pretty scenario, to be sure, but perhaps an entirely necessary one.

Can an instructor use student witnesses to substantiate an account of an incident of disruption?

Yes. By all means. An instructor may enlist the assistance of any and all eyewitnesses to incidents of disruption at any point in the disciplinary process. For example, if a student in a class has witnessed the misconduct of another student and volunteers to provide testimony to the acts of disruption, that student can submit in writing to the instructor his or her observations. The student's written account can then be incorporated into the report that is eventually transmitted to the designated administrator by the instructor. If willing, the student can also later serve as a witness for the instructor at the disciplinary hearing in which the alleged misconduct will be duly investigated and adjudicated. The reliable testimonies of others, authenticating your own observations, ordinarily will augment the credibility of your allegations and thereby fortify your petition for disciplinary sanctions.

There are several provisos that should be heeded if you are considering enlisting students as witnesses in a disciplinary procedure. First, students should be entirely free to decline to serve as witnesses without fear of academic or disciplinary reprisals from instructors. Second, they should be encouraged to seek advice, legal or otherwise, regarding the advisability of serving as witnesses. Finally, the college should extend to witnesses whatever safeguards are necessary to fully protect them from reprisals at the hands of the student against whom they are about to testify.

At what point should an instructor involve an administrator in investigating a disciplinary matter?

Usually, it is a good idea to involve an administrator if you have had to dismiss a student from your classroom for misconduct. Also, if a student's misconduct leads you to believe that criminal charges are warranted, this would definitely be cause to file a disciplinary report. A disciplinary report is probably in order if a previous in-the-classroom form of discipline as been ineffective. And, if the disruptive behavior has, for any reason, caused the classroom to become a hostile, untenable environment, file a disciplinary report. Finally, if you suspect that the disruptive behavior warrants suspension or expulsion, you should file a disciplinary report.

Students who belong to violent gangs worry me. Some of them wear jackets and emblems on campus that denote gang membership. Is there anything that can be done about students who belong to gangs that perpetrate violent crimes in the community?

The fact that students wear jackets and emblems that signify their membership in a gang, even a gang notorious for its violence, does not in itself suggest cause for alarm. Most students who engage in delinquencies and crimes in the community do not repeat those offenses while on the campus of the college. For example, there are thousands of students attending colleges throughout this country who are each day in their own communities engaging in such crimes as domestic violence, rape, theft, drug trafficking, assault, and even murder, yet while they are on the property of the college campus their behavior is, rather anomalously, pretty straitlaced. The explanation for this seeming anomaly is fairly obvious: they want to get an education and do not want to jeopardize this goal by running afoul of college authorities by engaging in misconduct while on campus. In any event, instructors should not assume that student toughs who advertise their gang memberships through the jackets and emblems they wear will perpetrate antisocial acts on campus.

There are, however, several factors to be considered whenever students who belong to notoriously violent gangs appear on campus, especially in significant numbers. College authorities may need to be alert to the possibility that these students will exert, overtly or subliminally, interpersonal pressure upon other students to submit to their demands. Thus, gang members may, as they are wont to do in the community, engage in acts of physical intimidation and extortion in order to establish their tyranny over other students. Obviously, if college authorities detect such a dangerous trend, it should be thwarted at once.

Also, if gang members (or, for that matter, any other students) engage in serious misconduct in off-campus settings (such as athletic events, concerts, dances, etc.) that are sponsored by and are under the auspices of the college, their misconduct is likely to be subject to the college's code of student conduct and therefore is punishable.

It is probably worth mentioning in this context that courts of law in this country are incrementally extending the authority of educational institutions to hold their students accountable for their off-campus behavior (and, I might add, are also extending in the process their potential legal liability). For example, a high school student was recently suspended because he was found guilty of using his home computer to harass another student. Because the victim was in dread of having this young man in school with her, she complained, and the school, in deference to her fears, suspended him. At this writing, the school has withstood a legal challenge to its actions in this case. Thus, extrapolating from the trend of such legal precedents, it is possible that students (such as gang members) who have harassed or injured fellow students in the community could have their academic status adversely affected by their off-campus misconduct **if the college can satisfactorily demonstrate that the off-campus misconduct will have a harmful affect upon their other students, especially if the victims are expected to be in the proximity of the perpetrator while on campus.** Campus authorities might keep this concept in mind, by the way, whenever they are considering allowing a suspected or convicted rapist to remain in close propinquity to the rape victim while they are on campus together.

There also seems to be a trend in the courts to allow colleges to discipline students for off-campus misconduct that detracts from or sullies the stature and reputation of the college. Thus, it is conceivable that a student could be legally disciplined by a college when convicted of, for example, the heinous off-campus crime of kidnapping and beating a child to death given the wide and shocking publicity that usually attends such crimes. Colleges who are tempted to discipline students for tarnishing their reputations by engaging in antisocial or criminal behavior in the community usually need to establish that a clear nexus exists between the student's misconduct and the palpable diminishment of the college's good name. In any case, I think colleges that attempt to argue that membership in a gang, however disreputable, is in itself a basis for disciplining a student because such membership tarnishes the reputation of the school will find themselves shipwrecked upon the shoals of formidable challenges in the courts based upon the likely unconstitutional of such a posture.

There are a few students in my class who tend to monopolize our discussions with irrelevant and prolonged remarks about their favorite causes. Quite often their long monologues become highly personal or ideological. What do you suggest?

It is important for instructors to maintain reasonable control over the course of classroom discussions. Although students may be encouraged to speak freely and at length, they may also need to be reminded to keep their comments limited to the subject under discussion and to avoid interminable speechifying.

Some students may be inclined to use the classroom as a forum to trumpet their favorite personal or political ideology. Others might use it as one might use a psychotherapist's couch, namely, to air their innermost thoughts and beliefs or to heedlessly disclose intimate information about their personal lives. Generally, such students need, first, to be firmly blocked from endlessly diverting classroom discussions into irrelevant arenas. Instructors can do this by simply and politely telling the students that they have used up their allotted time and now it is some else's turn to speak. If the student's remarks are entirely nongermane to the subject under discussion, that fact can be pointed out along with reminders to return to the topic of the day.

Students who indulge themselves by giving long-winded orations in class or by personalizing all subjects through sharing intimate information about their personal lives, do so, quite often, because they have acute needs for attention and recognition. Sometimes, however, some students employ this form of disruptive behavior as a ruse with which they can cover up their lack of knowledge about the coursework. In other words, if they can't grasp the material under discussion, they will create their own material or agenda. Regardless of the basic motivations of students either to monopolize or personalize classroom discussions, this form of behavior is disruptive and unacceptable, and therefore should be blocked and prohibited. After all, most instructors know that most of their students will wholeheartedly resent them if they do not do something affirmative to harness the garrulity of some of their classmates.

If students, after they have been repeatedly reminded or warned to curtail the irrelevancy and/or span of their remarks, continue to disrupt classroom discussions in this manner, it may be time to report them to an administrator for disciplinary intervention.

To be frank, I wish to be liked by my students. Not because it will look good on an evaluation, but because I enjoy the feeling of being appreciated for my work. How can I discipline a student and still expect to be liked by that student?

There are several ways to answer this question. First, as I have stated elsewhere, students who are disciplined by instructors will usually feel that the discipline, however proportionate to the infraction, is unfair, unwarranted, and unnecessary. Therefore, at least for a while, the average student who is disciplined will dislike the instructor, perhaps quite intensely. Therefore, instructors will need to be thick-skinned and stout-hearted whenever they impose discipline because they are likely in such instances to be accused of having such vices as personal bias, incompetence, impaired judgment, and vengeful intentions. If you are reasonably confident that the discipline is warranted and proportionate and is not animated by some personal animus for the student, it is usually wise to stand firm behind the disciplinary measure. To cave in to the student's barrage of ugly characterizations of your motives and level of professional competency, whether out of guilt or a wish to be liked, by rescinding the disciplinary measure, is a recipe for big-time trouble. It is likely that the disruptive student will have learned from your ready acquiescence that attacks upon your character and judgment will in the future neutralize your ability to exercise your rightful authority to prohibit classroom misconduct. In other words, your excessive passivity will hand the disruptive student a license for engaging in further misconduct and, additionally, may well open the floodgates for mischief from other students who have witnessed this miscarriage of justice. Obviously, such a serious risk should not, if you can help it, be bartered for the dubious reward of being liked by a disruptive student.

Instructors who worry about being disliked by a student they are about to discipline probably should ask themselves whether their concerns are misguided and misplaced. If a student is disrespectful and contemptuous enough to repeatedly engage in disruptive behavior, is this the kind of person whose affection and appreciation should be coveted by an instructor? Instructors might find it helpful and even liberating to understand that some disruptive students are capable of liking their teachers only if they kowtow to their selfish and tyrannical demands. Winning the affection of some disruptive students, then, may entail the forfeiture of a far more important and cherished goal; namely, maintaining one's self-respect, high standards, and professional integrity while earning the respect and affection of those students who have the good sense to appreciate such qualities in their instructors.

An important factor that should always be considered when one frets over the possibility of engendering dislike in a disruptive student is the even greater likelihood that a failure to discipline a disruptive student will engender intense dislike for the instructor among most of the other students in the class, who prefer, as they should, to learn in a classroom environment untrammeled by disruption. Thus, to anguish over whether a disruptive student may dislike you for using discipline while ignoring the possibility that you will invite the animosity of your other students (who are respectfully non-disruptive) if you do not use discipline, is a gainless form of soul-searching.

Finally, when considering the matter of being disliked by disruptive students, instructors might keep in mind something they already know about the process of learning; namely, that learning new concepts, ideas, and modes of thinking can be a very slow and painfully difficult intellectual and emotional process and therefore is often met with hostile resistance by many students. Therefore, some students may need considerable time and assistance in order to assimilate new ideas and perspectives.

The same principle holds true for many students when it comes to the matter of disruptive behavior. A persistently disruptive student must, in order to adapt to the college environment, unlearn unacceptable forms of misconduct while replacing them with socially sanctioned forms of behavior. It is to be expected that, for some disruptive students, this will be a formidable if not impossible task. The instructor who disciplines a disruptive student, then, should expect an initial response of hostile resistance and dislike. However, like other forms of learning, some disruptive students may **in time** come to appreciate the fact that they have, by being disciplined for misconduct, been taught something of vital importance, perhaps something that will even help them salvage their college career and place them in good stead with others in the future. Thus, when considering the matter of whether a disruptive student will dislike them for using discipline, instructors might do well to put aside the drama of the moment and think instead of the long-term benefit the student may derive from learning something constructive from the experience of having been disciplined for misconduct. Although it may now be of little mental comfort to you to imagine that students might, twenty or thirty years later, appreciate and actually like you for having once prohibited them from disturbing others, it is nevertheless a conception worth considering. If, on the other hand, a student still hates you twenty years later, you will probably have more important things to worry about, such as planning your retirement.

What should be done about a student who walks into class wearing a T-shirt with the words "Fuck you" emblazoned on it? I find it offensive and so do many of my other students. Do I have a right to prohibit this form of attire?

In responding to this question, I will quote from what I had written about this subject in my earlier book, *Coping with the Disruptive College Student: A Practical Model.*

In recent years colleges have certainly relaxed their standards regarding the language and dress of students. Anyone who spends any time moseying about the average college campus will hear many students and college employees use obscenities and vulgarisms with relative abandon. With some exceptions, such as at some religiously oriented or private schools, the language and dress of students are extended extremely wide latitude. Under the First Amendment, the right of free speech is vastly protected. But is that right absolute on the college campus?

Apparently not. Without undertaking an extensive review of court decisions on these matters, suffice it so say that students at public institutions of higher education enjoy rather unlimitedly free, constitutionally protected, political speech. However, public educational institutions can abridge a student's speech or dress in the following situations:

1. If the student's speech or dress demonstrably and adversely affects the health and safety of other members of the college community and;

2. If the student's speech demonstrably leads to a breach of the peace or seriously disrupts the educational processes of the college.

I know of another case similar to your own. Evidently, this student's dress was not considered problematic until a female classmate registered a complaint, alleging that the epithet was a form of sexual harassment. The student who wore the epithetic T-shirt, when confronted with his classmate's allegation of sexual harassment and encouraged to relinquish the shirt, rejoined with the argument that it was his constitutional right to express himself in this manner. Fortunately, in recent years women's legal protections against harassment have been broadened by prevailing law. Acutely aware of this fact, the administrator handling this matter was at his wit's end trying to decide whose legal rights should prevail in this sticky case.

He was advised in the following manner: 1) To seek legal advice from his college attorney and 2) To spend more time with the two disputants on an informal basis, appealing to their sense of fair play and goodwill, and to the overriding need for compromise in such conflictual situations. Perhaps, too, friends or other persons who know and are trusted by the disputants could intercede and play a constructive role in mollifying them and resolving the crisis.

Sometimes, when college officials become overly anxious about a legal dispute between students and a prospective lawsuit against the college, they lose sight of the need to approach contentious students in a non-authoritative and even-tempered manner. Subtly, but significantly, contentious students often sense how much they unnerve instructors and administrators with their offensive behavior and their litigious threats and, as a result, they themselves become even more hostile and intransigent. Often, indefatigable patience, humor, and a good dose of lively imagination will enable instructors and administrators to resolve and weather such crises far more than an immediate and dire invocation of laws and regulations.

In sum, if you have serious doubts about the use of discipline in a case involving offensive attire, consult your administrator for advice and intervention. Administrators usually have more ready access to legal counsel than instructors and, moreover, may in the final analysis be the only college officials with the legally constituted authority to effectively resolve such situations.

I had a student in my class last semester whose disruptive behavior I did not report. Is it now too late? Is there a "statute of limitations" that governs such situations?

Statutes of limitations do exist on many college campuses with respect to disciplinary matters. They vary in length, but at some schools instructors may have as many as five or more years during which they can retroactively document and report incidents of disruption.

Of course, the sooner one documents and reports a prior incident of disruption, the greater the likelihood of a successful petition for discipline. Ancient documentation may suffer from the attenuation of accurate and reliable information regarding the disruptive incident. Also, in the intervening months or years, witnesses who might have provided vital testimony at the time of the incident, may disperse from sight, thus vitiating the credibility of your allegations.

If you are in doubt about time constraints that may govern your petition for a disciplinary investigation, consult your designated administrator for clarification.

What are some ways to keep your cool when dealing with disruptive students? I sometimes find it hard to keep my temper under control.

Naturally, losing one's temper is apt to make a bad situation much worse. As well, instructors who lose their tempers when dealing with a disruptive student may later be justifiably charged with having instigated or at least aggravated the disruptive crisis.

Instructors who lose control of their tempers do so for a variety of reasons. Some simply have a short fuse. However, if your own fuse is of sufficient length as to allow you time to blueprint a strategy for intervention, I would suggest the following approach. Take heed of your own emotional state as you are encountering disruptive behavior. If a student's misconduct is beginning to ruffle your feathers, it is probably the time to intervene with a warning. If you do not intervene and the misconduct continues, you are likely to find yourself feeling like a seething cauldron. This is probably a measure of the extent to which you are allowing yourself (and your other students) to be victimized by the disruptive student.

Although you have probably already passed the point at which you could have most appropriately intervened, it is far from being too late. Your tension and fury are emotional proclamations that call for release from and resolution of an abusively disruptive situation. This release, if you can help it, should not be in the form of a loud, vituperative, and blistering sermon. It usually is quite sufficient to voice disapproval of disruptive behavior in quiet, respectful but firm tones and in language that specifically addresses the inappropriateness of the misconduct. If these verbal warnings are ineffectual, they should be coupled with written warnings and, if necessary, a petition for administrative intervention.

By eliminating disruptive behavior quickly and decisively you will be removing the source of your rage and should have little difficulty controlling your temper thereafter. Also, by taking decisive steps to abate misconduct you will have changed your behavior from passive and inactive to proactive and affirmative. Generally, proactive and positively assertive behavior releases aggression while a passive stance in the face of abusive misconduct tends to stoke the fires of angry emotions. Therefore, if you discover that you are in the throes of stoically enduring abusive misconduct day after day in your classroom and hating the thought of coming to work because the classroom has become a hellish torture chamber, it behooves you to find some way to rid yourself of your self-destructive stoicism by taking affirmative action to prohibit and eliminate the misconduct as soon as possible. If you do this successfully, you will probably have few concerns about outbursts of temper.

When should I consider referring a disruptive student to a counselor or psychotherapist?

A disruptive student can be referred to a counseling or psychotherapy service at any time; however, there are several factors to be considered before such a referral takes place. First, the purpose of the referral should be clear to both the instructor and the student. For example, if the primary purpose of the referral is to correct or remedy the student's disruptive behavior, the referral will probably lack sufficient legitimacy and merit. Such a referral will probably entail having the instructor relinquish important disciplinary prerogatives (e.g., the authority to set and enforce behavioral standards) while assigning to a counselor the responsibility to serve as an agent of social control. This type of referral normally results in an institutional anomaly that places the counselor, whose official job it is to heal and guide, in the role of quasi-disciplinarian and in the process abrogates the instructor's authority to serve in the legitimate and absolutely essential role of disciplinarian. Clearly, this is not a sensible way to do business.

It is also usually inappropriate to refer a disruptive student for counseling if such a referral is an obvious substitute for discipline. Even when such a referral is animated by an altruistic wish to be kind and gentle with a disruptive student, it sends a misleading and garbled message to the student. It conveys the erroneous notion that the nub of the disruptive problem is not the student's misconduct but rather some arcane disarray in the student's psyche. Although it may indeed be true that the student's misconduct is a manifestation of a serious mental disorder or, perhaps, of a more pedestrian form of stress, we should not lose sight of the fact that in dealing with a disruptive student the most important and achievable goal is to correct that student's **behavior.** It is clearly not realistic, wise, or appropriate to seek to effect characterologic changes in disruptive students through referrals to counselors or psychotherapists.

The student who pursues such a referral may do so simply to get a "monkey" off his or her back, that is, to simply placate the instructor. Or, even if that student undertakes therapy with a serious intent to change, intrapsychically and behaviorally, the process of change may take many months or even years. In the meantime the disruptive behavior may persist or even get worse. And, let us not lose sight of the real possibility that the therapy could fail and the patient will get decidedly worse, at least behaviorally.

Before referring students for counseling or therapy it is usually advisable to assess the student's openness to such assistance. There are of course some students who will take umbrage with an instructor who makes such a referral because they interpret the instructor's assistive goad to be malevolently motivated and stigmatizing. In such cases, the student might accuse the instructor of falsely identifying him or her as a crazy person. This obviously can result in a very fractious and nasty encounter. Students who are receptive to such referrals usually indicate their receptivity by bringing up the subject of therapy or their need for professional help. It is at that point that instructors might capitalize upon the moment by asking if they can be of assistance with a referral. If the student adamantly declines, it is probably best to drop the subject. If the student accepts the offer, it is probably advisable, before carrying out the referral, to ask if the student is already in therapy. If the student already has a therapist, rather than the run the risk of offering the student a redundancy of services, an instructor can simply respect that student's relationship with his or her current therapist by not tampering with it.

Finally, when referring a student to a counselor or a therapist, it is essential that there be no "or else" quality to your communication. In other words, it should be made abundantly clear to the student that there will be no academic penalty for declining therapy nor will there be a reward (say, in the form of a mitigation of disciplinary sanctions) for accepting the referral. This can be stated to the student in the following terms: "Your behavior in my class has been unacceptable. I have given you a warning about it and if your misconduct is repeated I will report the matter to an administrator for disciplinary intervention. Since you've indicated an interest in receiving therapy, I will be happy to give you the information you need in order to find a therapist. However, you should understand that, whether you undertake therapy or not, your behavior in my class must conform to the code of student conduct. If it does not, being in therapy will not get you off the hook. I must insist upon acceptable behavior in order to teach the course."

Is an instructor permitted to penalize a student for poor attendance by reducing the student's grade?

It is generally permissible to reduce a student's grade as a penalty for substandard attendance. After all, participation in class discussions and verbal responses to an instructor's comments and questions are often reliable indices of the student's level of acquired knowledge.

There are, however, several conditions that should be met before an instructor imposes academic penalties for unacceptable attendance. First, these penalties should be spelled out in the course syllabus. This will help to obviate the disagreeable possibility that the academic penalty will shock and insult the student. When penalties come as a shock and an insult they invite retaliation, sometimes in the form of valid criticisms that the instructor, by providing no forewarning to the student, behaved peremptorily and unfairly.

Second, penalties for poor attendance should be standardized, that is, they should be applied evenly to all students. This, of course, will decidedly enhance the possibility that the academic penalty will be imposed in a non-discriminatory manner.

Third, instructors who impose academic penalties for poor attendance should certainly do their utmost to bring their own attendance and punctuality up to snuff. This is not just a matter of practicing what you preach. If you discipline a student for poor attendance and your own attendance is in the same dismal league, there is a fair chance that the student can persuasively claim that his or her poor attendance is the result of a reasonable expectation that you will not show up when you are expected. This, I would guess, can be a compelling defense.

Finally, when imposing penalties for poor attendance, instructors should be on the lookout for extenuating or extraordinary circumstances that might mitigate these penalties. For both humanitarian and legal reasons, extenuating circumstances, such as the death of a parent, should be carefully weighed before meting out penalties. Perhaps, in the event of an extenuating circumstance, the student can redress the attendance problem by, for example, doing extra assignments.

Are there times when it is appropriate for instructors to conduct background checks on students to determine if they have criminal records? Are these records available to the general public?

There are times when a background check might not only be appropriate but, from a legal standpoint, would be entirely essential. For example, students who are enrolled in nursing and police science courses are entering careers for which a prior criminal record might be a disqualifying factor. If such students complete these courses without a background check and later attempt to find employment in these

Coping with Misconduct in the College Classroom

fields, they may then discover that their prior crimes have deemed them ineligible and, sadly, all the time and work they put into their college courses has been for naught. To make matters worse, they probably took the seats of other students who would be entirely qualified to enter these fields.

Criminal records of adults are accessible to the public. The criminal records of juveniles are not. Nor are the records of arrests without conviction.

If an instructor seeks to vet a student's criminal record for the purpose of predicting classroom behavior, it is well to realize that this is a precarious and possibly fruitless venture. Criminal records usually reflect a person's antisociality in the community, not on a college campus. The way a person behaves in the community or in a volatile domestic situation may have little correlation to how that person comports himself or herself while on the campus. To use an extreme example, a criminal background check might uncover the gruesome fact that the student was a convicted killer. Does this necessarily mean that the student is a menace to the campus community? Strangely, it does not. It is entirely possible that the hospitable and nurturing qualities of campus life will have a subduing affect upon the student and help to balm his savage impulses. Naturally, a person who knows of the student's career as a violent killer would be dull-witted to step off the campus with him or her or enter secluded areas on the campus with such an individual. My only point, however, is to suggest that criminal records are not always sound prognosticators of how students will behave within the milieu of academia.

There is one particular way in which a criminal record might be of invaluable practical assistance. If a student engages in threatening or menacing behavior and it is discovered that he or she has a long criminal history of violence toward others, it behooves the college to take strong, affirmative measures to ensure that the student will not inflict harm upon staff or students. Keeping the student's violent history in mind, the college may elect to call the police or expel the student before there is a general outbreak of mayhem to contend with.

You obviously have a bias in favor of using discipline over psychotherapy in handling disruptive students. Can you explain why?

Discipline has many decided advantages over psychotherapy for coping with disruptive students. First, it is a far superior procedure with which to awaken the disruptive student to the consequences of serious misconduct. The student who is disciplined for misconduct will readily feel the distressful impact of a loss of academic privileges. Thus, he or she must face a clear, unavoidable moral choice: to comply with the codes of student conduct or infract those codes and incur the further deprivation of privileges. Given this clear moral choice, even the most rambunctious student is likely to think twice before risking penalties for misconduct.

Psychotherapy, on the other hand, normally does not entail such moral choices. Although disruptive students may not like the prospect of giving up an hour a week to unbosom their emotions to a complete stranger, they otherwise sacrifice very little when they undergo psychotherapy. Thus, if therapy is used as a substitute for discipline, it is not likely that the experience will inculcate in the student an awareness that misconduct can and should entail adverse consequences. As a matter of fact, in cases where psychotherapy is proffered as an alternative to discipline, the opposite moral lesson may be inferred: to wit, if one engages in misconduct one is rewarded with the benign experience of discussing it with a caring professional. In other words, the offer of psychotherapy might inadvertently foster and abet further misconduct.

Second, discipline, when it is used effectively, works quickly, decisively, and correctively. The student soon ceases to disrupt the classroom and the instructor can go about the business of teaching in an untrammeled atmosphere. By contrast, psychotherapy ordinarily takes considerable time to plumb the roots of a person's emotional conflicts and maladaptive behavior. In some cases, even after many months or years of psychotherapy, an antisocial person may remain immovably entrenched in disruptive modes of behavior. As a colleague in the mental health field once pointed out, many highly disruptive students are "externalizers." They are impulsive, act out their hostile urges and impulses, demonstrate little capacity for introspection, and have an underdeveloped conscience. Given their psychological makeup, many of our highly disruptive students are very poor candidates for psychotherapy, a process that usually requires a reasonable tolerance for frustration and ambiguity, a fairly developed introspective capability and a conscience that can clearly distinguish between right and wrong.

Finally, it is important, I think, to keep in mind that when a student is disruptive our primary goal should be to prohibit and eliminate the misconduct, not transform the student's character or personality. Discipline, if used properly, is perfectly designed to achieve the goal of prohibiting and eliminating misconduct. Psychotherapy is not, and should not be, designed to control social misconduct. It is, of course, possible that a positive by-product of psychotherapy will be the diminution of the student's misconduct. However, a psychotherapist who conducts the therapy with the express purpose of curtailing a student's misconduct is carrying out an illegitimate (and mostly likely fruitless) mission and is thereby bastardizing the essential role and value of the psychotherapeutic enterprise: to heal and guide.

One final caveat. The procedures of discipline and psychotherapy need not be viewed as mutually exclusive or antagonistic. A student may enter therapy with the genuine desire to overcome violent or disruptive tendencies that have led to troublesome encounters with college authorities. By all means, this student should be provided with therapy. However, it should be borne in mind that the goal of correcting and eliminating the misconduct is the student's, not the therapist's or the institution's. This is a vital distinction because it forces everyone to recognize that it is the student's responsibility to overcome the problem of his or her disruptive behavior, not the therapist's or the institution's. Furthermore, under most circumstances it is also the student's inalienable right to refuse to undergo psychotherapy but **it is never the student's right to engage in serious misconduct.** These are all-important moral lessons that should be conveyed by the authorities who administer discipline as well as those who conduct psychotherapy on the college campus.

Before concluding this discussion about therapy and discipline I would like to make one final point. It is entirely valid, in my view, to regard psychotherapy as a procedure that will catalyze psychological change and, if it is effective, will lead to enhanced self-awareness and improved interpersonal behavior. It is also true, despite the fact that it seems to be only murkily understood by many college employees, that a just and effective disciplinary system will also catalyze positive psychological and behavioral changes.

Simply described, a sound disciplinary system will first emotionally **awaken** a disruptive student to the consequences of his or her misconduct. This, however, is only the first phase of a complex psychological process. If the use of discipline to correct disruptive behavior is successful (that is, it quells the student's disruptiveness), the student may begin to **identify** with the purposes, objectives, and positive value of the discipline; namely, to permit other students to learn and teachers to teach in an optimally disruption-free environment. If a formerly disruptive student can, as an intermediate step, identify with the value of respectful interpersonal conduct, he or she may then complete the psychological cycle by emotionally **internalizing** the principles and values that underlie the codes of student conduct. By internalizing these values—that is, allowing these values to become an organic part of oneself—the student will have been transformed into a more regardful and dignified member of the academic community. Obviously, any formerly disruptive student who accomplishes such an important moral and psychological transformation deserves considerable credit and recognition. I do not think it is Pollyanish or Utopian to expect that the creative, just, and timely use of disciplinary procedures can produce such positive results with a great many students.

In sum, my bias in favor of disciplinary measures in handling disruptive students is based upon my conviction that the disruptive student who incurs a disciplinary procedure is likely to undergo a **psychological** experience of a truly positive transformative nature that is more immediate and profound than can be achieved through counseling or psychotherapy.

CENTER FOR TEACHING EXCELLENCE
Canisius College

		DATE DUE	

CENTER FOR TEACHING EXCELLENCE
Canisius College